First Edition 2005

Poetry and Prose of the Tang and Song

Translated by
Yang Xianyi and Gladys Yang

CONFUCIUS INSTITUTE
at Colorado State University

Printed in China

© Foreign Languages Press, Beijing, China, 2005

Published by Foreign Languages Press
24 Baiwanzhuang Road, Beijing 100037, China

E-mail Address: info@flp.com.cn
sales@flp.com.cn

China International Book Trading Corporation
35 Chegongzhuang Xilu, Beijing 100044, China
Beijing, China

Printed in the People's Republic of China

Pand

First Edition 2005

ISBN 7-119-03855-7
©Foreign Languages Press, Beijing, China, 2005
Published by Foreign Languages Press
24 Baiwanzhuang Road, Beijing 100037, China
Website: http://www.flp.com.cn
E-mail Address: info@flp.com.cn
sales@flp.com.cn
Distributed by China International Book Trading Corporation
35 Chegongzhuang Xilu, Beijing 100044, China
P.O. Box 399, Beijing, China
Printed in the People's Republic of China

CONTENTS

Publisher's Note

THE Tang (618-907) and Song (960-1279) dynasties, spanning more than 600 years, saw a period of great economic and cultural development in Chinese society. During this golden age of classical literature, numerous masterpieces were written which have exerted a profound influence ever since.

Tang-dynasty poetry can be divided into three periods, early, middle and late Tang, which correspond to the rise and decline of the dynasty.

In the early period from 618-712, classical poetry began to change from the euphuistic, formalistic style into a more vigorous one. Wang Bo, Yang Jiong, Lu Zhaolin and Luo Binwang were the four greatest poets of the period. They were not limited to the forms of court poetry but also commented on society. They played an influential role in changing the poetical trend.

The middle Tang period was from 713-770, when many great Tang poets emerged, finally establishing the new form of classical poetry. Social life was reflected in all its aspects by these poets, and this period is considered the peak of Tang poetic achievement. Famous poets of this period are Meng Haoran and Wang Wei who described country life and Gao Shi and Cen Shen who dealt with life at the frontier. But it is the appearance of immortal poets like Li Bai and Du Fu that made Tang poetry of this period significant. With their genius, passionate love for their country and the people and their deep understanding of life, they developed their own styles and created poems which reflected this great period in Chinese history. They are considered as the greatest of all Chinese classical poets.

A new upsurge in Tang poetry began with the movement to write critical poems as advocated by Bai Juyi and Yuan Zhen. They called these "new *yuefu* songs." Seeing the rottenness of the society, the corruption in politics and the miseries of the masses, these poets wished to develop the realist tradition in poetry so that literature dealt with topical subjects and served society. They were opposed to empty laments merely expressing personal feelings. As in the case of Du Fu, the titles of his poems expressed the content, which was a break with traditional *yuefu* song titles. The efforts of Bai Juyi and Yuan Zhen established the foundation of this new movement.

Late Tang poetry can be divided into two periods. In the early period the most famous poets were Li Shangyin and Du Mu. After the two poets, Tang poetry declined, becoming imitative and less original.

Besides poetry, prose writing in the Tang Dynasty was also noteworthy. The famous Tang-dynasty classicist movement was both an important ideological reform and a literary reform. It advocated learning from classical prose and was opposed to the ornate and euphuistic style predominant in the early Tang period. Representative writers of the classicist movement are Han Yu and Liu Zongyuan, whose major works are selected into this book.

The classicist movement continued in the Song Dynasty to fight against the revived euphuistic style. The most famous prose writers of this period include Ouyang Xiu, Su Shi, Su Xun, Su Che, Wang Anshi and Zeng Gong. Together with Han Yu and Liu Zongyuan of the Tang Dynasty, they were called the Eight Great Masters of the Tang and Song Dynasties.

Song Dynasty also enjoyed the flourishing of the *ci* poetry, which first appeared in the late Tang Dynasty. *Among the Flowers* was a famous early tenth-century collection of *ci* poems written by the literati on the theme of love and sorrow of departing. Later poets in the Song Dynasty enlarged the themes to describe scenery, expound certain philosophies and introduce classical lore. Famous Song-dynasty *ci* poets include Xin Qiji, Su Shi, Zhou Bangyan, and Jiang Kui, who each has left several hundred *ci* poems.

This collection of *Poetry and Prose of the Tang and Song* is only a small sample of the voluminous literature of the Tang and Song dynasties. However, in its variety, it should prove informative and interesting for specialist and general readers alike.

Wang Wei

Wang Wei (701-761 or 698-759) was from Qixian County in Shanxi. He embarked upon an official career at an early age and in his later years retired to his country home in Lantian County, southeast of present-day Xi'an. A great painter and an accomplished musician, Wang for many represents the classical ideal of the cultured scholar-official. The majority of his poems are about nature and are written in a restrained, exquisite and deeply symbolic style.

Wei River Farm

A village in the setting sun;
Down humble lanes the cows and sheep wind home;
An old man, waiting for a shepherd boy,
Leans on his staff beside his wicker gate.
Pheasants are crying, wheat is in the ear;
Silkworms are dormant, sparse the mulberry leaves;
Up come two farmers shouldering their hoes
And meeting fall to talking. . .
Till, envying their carefree life,
I chant the sad old song *Longing for Home*. *

The Countryside After Rain

FRESH washed by rain the rolling plain,
No mist or dust as far as eye can see;
A gate in the stockade gives on the ford,
The village trees verge on the valley's head;
White water gleams beyond the fields
And green peaks loom behind the hills;
A busy season, this, for farming folk;
Whole families are tilling the southern fields.

---

* From the *Book of Songs*.

Passing the Monastery of Gathered Fragrance

WHERE is it, the Monastery of Gathered Fragrance?
Mile after mile I climb the cloudy peaks;
Here are old trees, a path that no man treads
And deep in the hills the sound of a temple bell;
A fountain chokes on jagged rocks,
Among these dark green pines the sun seems chill;
I come at twilight to a deep pool —
Can the monk at his devotions curb the evil dragon?

An Autumn Evening in the Hills

THROUGH empty hills new washed by rain
As dusk descends the autumn comes;
Bright moonlight falls through pines,
Clear springs flow over stones;
The bamboos rustle as girls return from washing,
Lotus flowers stir as a fishing boat casts off;
Faded the fragrance of spring,
Yet, friend, there is enough to keep you here.

My Retreat by the Zhongnan Mountains

MIDWAY through life I set my heart on Truth
And have come to end my days by the Southern Hills;
When the mood takes me I stroll out alone,
My pleasure shared by none.
I walk to where streams rise,
Sit watching as the clouds drift up the sky,
And meeting with an old man in the woods
Talk and laugh with him, forgetting to return.

Living in the Hills

IN solitude I close my wooden gate,
As shadows fall I watch the setting sun;
The cranes have made their nests among the pines,
And to my rustic door few callers come;
Fresh powder dusts the young bamboo,
Its faded petals the red lotus sheds;
At the ferry landing lights spring up
And girls laden with water-chestnuts come flocking home.

The Zhongnan Mountains

NEAR the celestial capital, Taiyi*
Marches range after range to meet the sea;
Far off I glimpse it shrouded in white clouds,
And a blue haze, fading as soon as seen;
Its central peak divides the regions round,
Shadow and sunlight sunder its far valleys;
Seeking some lodging for the night,
I hail the woodcutter across the stream.

Watching the Hunt

A gusty wind, twang of horn-backed bows:
The general is hunting at Weicheng;
Hawks' eyes are keen above the withered grass,
Horse-hooves fall lightly where the snow has melted;
They wheel past Xinfeng Market
And head home to the camp at Xiliu,
Turning once to mark where the vulture fell:
The plain sweeps far off to the evening clouds.

---

* The highest peak of the Zhongnan Mountains.

A View of the Han River

THE three rivers of Xiang meet in the land of Chu;
Through the gateway of Jing the nine tributaries flow;
The river sweeps beyond the earth and sky,
Half visible the hills and half unseen;
Towns seem afloat upon the bank ahead,
Waves are rocking the distant sky;
A fine day like this in Xiangyang
And the old hermit will get happily drunk!

My Mission to the Frontier

A single carriage sets off for the border,
Journeying past the subject state of Juyan;
On we jolt, leaving Han fortresses behind,
A wild goose winging back to the Hunnish sky.
In the great desert one straight plume of smoke,
By the long river at sunset a ball of flame;
Before Xiao Pass we meet a mounted patrol
And learn that our forces have taken Mount Yanran.

The Deer Enclosure

EMPTY the hills, no man in sight,
Yet voices echo here;
Deep in the woods slanting sunlight
Falls on the jade-green moss.

The Magnolia Enclosure

THE autumn hills glean the last light of day
As winged birds chase their mates,
Their vivid colours flash across the green,
Through drifting evening mist.

The Luan Family Rapids

IN spattering autumn rain
Over the rocks the swirling rapids plunge;
The leaping water sprinkles all around,
Startled into flight, the white egret alights again.

The Bamboo Lodge

SEATED alone by shadowy bamboos
I strum my lyre and laugh aloud;
None knows that I am here, deep in the woods;
Only the bright moon comes to shine on me.

Hibiscus Valley

HIBISCUS high on the trees
Flaunt red in the hills;
To this secluded valley no man comes,
Yet the flowers bloom and fall year after year.

The Gully of Twittering Birds

IDLY I watch the cassia petals fall;
Silent the night and empty the spring hills;
The rising moon startles the mountain birds
Which twitter fitfully in the spring gully.

Asking for News of Home

FRIEND, come from home,
What home news do you bring?
The day you left had the winter plum
Before my latticed window burst into bloom?

In the Hills

FROM dwindling stream white stones emerge;
Frosty the day and few the crimson leaves;
No rain has fallen on the mountain path —
Men's clothes are soaked by the green solitude.

Seeing Yuan the Second Off on a Mission to Anxi

A morning shower in Weicheng has settled the light dust;
The willows by the hostel are fresh and green;
Come, drink one more cup of wine,
West of the pass you will meet no more old friends.

LI BAI

Li Bai (701-762) is one of the greatest names in Chinese literature. He is believed to have been born in Central Asia and there is ample evidence to indicate that he moved with his family to Sichuan when he was five. At the age of 25 he began travelling in the hope of meeting people of influence who would help him to realize his political ambitions and ideals. In 742 he was summoned to the Tang capital. In 755, Li joined the loyalist forces led by Prince Yong in an attempt to resist the An Lushan rebels. When the Prince was defeated, he was banished to Guizhou. He regained his freedom when an amnesty was declared. He used the conventional verse forms of the day and his poetry, which frequently contains a strong element of fantasy and the supernatural, is known for its lyrical, innovative imagery and great beauty of language.

Verses in the Old Style

GREAT carriages raise swirls of dust,
Darkening the fields at noon;
What golden plenty have these mighty eunuchs,
Whose mansions reach the clouds!
See them on their way to a cock-fight —
What magnificent headgear, what canopies!
The breath of their nostrils makes a double rainbow,
Folk by the roadside shake with fear.
Since the time of the wise old man who washed his ears, *
There is none to distinguish between Yao and Zhi. **

The Sichuan Road

WHAT heights!
It is easier to climb to Heaven
Than take the Sichuan Road.
Long ago Can Cong and Yu Fu founded the kingdom of Shu;
Forty-eight thousand years went by,

---

* Tradition has it that in the time of the sage king Yao, a hermit named Xu You
was offered a share in the government but considered the invitation so demeaning
that he at once washed his ears.

** According to legend, Yao was a paragon of virtue and Zhi a notorious brigand.

Yet no road linked it with the land of Qin.*

Westward from Taibai Mountain** a bird track

Wandered to the summit of Mount Emei;***

But not until brave men had perished in the great land-
   slide****

Were bridges hooked together in the air

And a path hacked through the rocks.

Above, high peaks turn back the sun's chariot drawn by six
   dragons;

Below, the charging waves are caught in whirlpools;

Not even yellow cranes dare fly this way,

Monkeys cannot leap those gorges.

At Green Mud Ridge the path winds back and forth,

With nine twists for every hundred steps.

Touching the stars, the traveller looks up and gasps,

Then sinks down, clutching his heart, to groan aloud.

Friend, when will you return from this westward journey?

This is a fearful way. You cannot cross these cliffs.

The only living things are birds crying in ancient trees,

Male wooing female up and down the woods,

---

* Shu, the old name for western Sichuan, was conquered by the kingdom of Qin in
   316 B.C.

** A mountain west of the capital, Chang'an.

*** A mountain in western Sichuan.

**** There is a legend that King Hui of Qin promised his five daughters to the prince
   of Shu. Five brave men were sent to fetch them. On the way back they met a
   huge serpent which fled into a cave. When they tried to pull it out, the mountain
   crumbled and the men and princesses perished. Since then a rocky path linked
   the two kingdoms.

And the cuckoo, weary of empty hills,

Singing to the moon.

It is easier to climb to heaven

Than take the Sichuan Road.

The mere telling of its perils blanches youthful cheeks.

Peak follows peak, each but a hand's breadth from the sky;

Dead pine trees hang head down into the chasms,

Torrents and waterfalls outroar each other,

Pounding the cliffs and boiling over rocks,

Booming like thunder through a thousand caverns.

What takes you, traveller, this long, weary way

So filled with danger?

Sword Pass* is steep and narrow,

One man could hold this pass against ten thousand;

And sometimes its defenders

Are not mortal men but wolves and jackals.

By day we dread the savage tiger, by night the serpent,

Sharp-fanged sucker of blood

Who chops men down like stalks of hemp.

The City of Brocade** may be a pleasant place,

But it is best to seek your home.

For it is easier to climb to heaven

Than take the Sichuan Road.

I gaze into the west, and sigh.

---

* In northern Sichuan, on the route to Shaanxi where the kingdom of Qin was.
** A name for Chengdu, the capital of Shu.

Fighting South of the City

LAST year we fought at the source of the Sangkan,
This year, along river-beds in the Pamirs;
We have washed our swords in the foam of Parthian seas,
And grazed our horses among the snows of Tianshan.
After campaigning ten thousand *li*,
Our men are weary and old.
Battle and carnage are to the Huns like ploughing,
White bones are the only crop in these yellow sands.
Where the House of Qin built the Great Wall against the
    tribesmen,
The House of Han kept the beacon fires ablaze —
And still they blaze;
There seems no end to the fighting.
In the wilderness men hack one another to pieces,
Riderless horses neigh madly to the sky;
Kites and crows tear out human entrails,
And fly with them and hang them
In branches of dead trees;
The blood of soldiers smears grass and brambles;
What use is a commander without his troops?
War is a fearful thing —
And the wise prince resorts to it only if he must.

Travelling Is Hard

CLEAR wine in golden goblets, ten thousand cash a cup,
And costly delicacies on jade platters.
Yet I spurn drinking and toss away my chopsticks,
Sword in hand, restless, I wonder what to do.
I want to cross the Yellow River, but it's ice-bound;
I want to climb the Taihang Mountains, but they are snow-
  covered.
So idly I fish by a limpid stream, *
Dreaming of sailing towards the sun. **
Travelling is hard! Travelling is hard!
So many crossroads; which to choose?
One day I'll skim the waves, blown by the wind,
With sails hoisted high, across the vast ocean.

---

 * Lü Shang used to fish by the Wei River before he met King Wen of Zhou and
   helped him to conquer the Shangs.
 ** Yi Yin before he was discovered by King Tang of Shang dreamed that he was
   sailing in a barge towards the sun.

Song of Inspector Ding *

YUNYANG** sends conscript labour to the Yangtse,
Both river banks are alive with men and trade;
When the buffaloes of Wu pant beneath the moon,***
It's weary work hauling boats!
The river water's too muddy to drink,
Thick silt fills half the pot;
When workmen chant the Inspector's Song,
Hearts break, tears fall like rain.
Ten thousand slave in the quarries,
But who will haul the stone to the river bank?
Look yonder at rocky Mang and Dang —****
What tears have fallen here since ancient times!

---

* A song with a doleful tune believed to date from the fifth century. Each line ends
  with the words "Inspector Ding".
** Present-day Danyang in Jiangsu Province. Conscript labour was used to carry
  stone from the quarries to the river and to tow the boats upstream.
*** i.e. in the worst heat of summer. The old kingdom of Wu was situated in the
  lower Yangtse Valley. The buffaloes there, sensitive to the heat, were said to
  mistake the moon for the sun.
**** Two hills in Jiangsu noted for their fine stone.

Thoughts in the Silent Night

Beside my bed a pool of light —
Is it hoarfrost on the ground?
I lift my eyes and see the moon,
I bend my head and think of home.

The Song of Green Water

GREEN water, bright autumn sun,
On South Lake they're gathering duckweed.
The lotus, so lovely they seem about to speak,
Fill the rowers with despair.

Thoughts in Spring

THE grass of Yan is green silk,
Dark hang the mulberry boughs of Qin.
While you, my lord, are longing to return,
Your handmaiden is breaking her heart at home.
Ah, why does the spring wind, a stranger,
Part the curtains of my bed?

Zi Ye's Song *

THE moon shines upon Chang'an city;
From all households the sound of pounding clothes. **
The autumn wind cannot blow away all longing and anguish
For our men beyond the Jade Pass. ***
When will the hordes of Huns be conquered,
So our husbands can return from their long expedition?

To Wang Lun ****

I'M on board; we're about to sail,
When there's stamping and singing on shore;
Peach Blossom Pool is a thousand feet deep,
Yet not so deep, Wang Lun, as your love for me.

---

* Zi Ye was a Jin-dynasty girl who composed this tune.
** Clothes were laundered by pounding them with a pestle. In autumn women would busy themselves with this before making winter clothes for their husbands.
*** The Jade Pass was situated in present-day Gansu Province. It was the gateway to Xinjiang and Central Asia.
**** When Li Bai was staying in Jingxian in present-day Anhui, Wang Lun often brought him good wine to drink and came to see him off when he left.

A Visit to Sky-Mother Mountain in a Dream, a Song of Farewell

SEA-FARERS tell of fairy isles;
Lost among mist and waves.
But the men of Yue* speak of Sky-Mother Mountain
Showing herself through rifts in shimmering clouds.
Sky-Mother soars to heaven, spans the horizon,
Towers over the Five Peaks** and the Scarlet Fortress;
While Sky-Terrace, four hundred and eighty thousand feet high,
Staggers southeastward before it.
So, longing in my dreams for Wu and Yue,
One night I flew over Mirror Lake under the moon;
The moon cast my shadow on the water
And travelled with me all the way to Yanxi.
The lodge of Lord Xie*** still remained
Where green waters swirled and the cry of apes was shrill;
Donning the shoes of Xie,
I climbed the dark ladder of clouds.
Midway, I saw the sun rise from the sea,

---

* The land of Yue lay in what is now the province of Zhejiang, the home of the famous mountains: Sky-Mother, Scarlet Fortress and Sky-Terrace.

** Five high mountains in China: Mount Tai, Mount Hua, Mount Heng, Mount Heng and Mount Song.

*** Xie Lingyun, a Jin-dynasty poet who was fond of mountaineering and made himself special hobnailed shoes for climbing.

Heard the Cock of Heaven crow. *

And my path twisted through a thousand crags,

Enchanted by flowers I leaned against a rock,

And suddenly all was dark.

Growling of bears and snarls of dragons echoed

Among the rocks and streams;

The deep forest appalled me, I shrank from the lowering
   cliffs;

Dark were the clouds, heavy with rain;

Waters boiled into misty spray;

Lightning flashed; thunder roared;

Peaks tottered, boulders crashed;

And the stone gate of a great cavern

Yawned open.

Below me, a bottomless void of blue,

Sun and moon gleaming on terraces of silver and gold;

With rainbows for garments, and winds for horses,

The lords of the clouds descended, a mighty host.

Phoenixes circled the chariots, tigers played cithers,

As the immortals went by, rank upon rank.

My heart was seized by fear and wonder,

And waking with a start I cried out,

For nothing was there except my mat and pillow —

Gone was the world of mists and clouds.

And so with the pleasures of this life;

All pass, as water flows eastward.

---

* According to Chinese mythology, this cock roosted on a great tree in the southeast. When the sun rose it crowed, and all the cocks in the world followed suit.

I leave you, friend — when shall I return?
I shall pasture white stags among green peaks
And ride to visit mountains famed in legend.
Would you have me bow my head before mighty princes,
Forgetting all the joy of my heart?

Seeing Meng Haoran* Off to Yangzhou from Yellow Crane Tower**

AT Yellow Crane Tower in the west
My old friend says farewell;
In the mist and flowers of spring
He goes down to Yangzhou;
Lonely sail, distant shadow,
Vanish in blue emptiness;
All I see is the great river
Flowing into the far horizon.

---

* A contemporary poet and good friend of Li Bai.
** On the bank of the Yangtse in present-day Wuhan.

To a Friend Departing

GREEN hills skirt the northern suburb;
A sparkling stream circuits the eastern city.
After our leave-taking in this place,
Like thistledown, you'll drift ten thousand *li*.
A wanderer is aimless like a floating cloud;
An old friend lingers like the setting sun.
We wave as you start on your way;
Our horses separated sadly neigh.

A Farewell to Li Yun in the Xie Tiao Pavilion*

YESTERDAY has passed and gone beyond recall;
Today worries and sorrows assail my mind.
Gazing at wild geese flying in the autumn wind,
Let us drink our fill in this high pavilion.
Here is one who writes with great scholarship;
His spirited style and poems compare with Xie Tiao.
Our lofty ambitions soar high;
Seeking to reach the moon in the sky.
Cut water with a sword, the water flows on;
Quench sorrow with wine, the sorrow increases.

---

* Li Yun, or Li Hua, was an editor in the imperial library and a friend of Li Bai. The Xie Tiao Pavilion was built by the poet Xie Tiao (464-499). It was situated in Xuancheng, Anhui Province.

In our lifetime, our wishes are unfulfilled;
Tomorrow, hair unbound, we'll sail away in a boat.

A Reply to Someone in the Mountains

YOU ask why I choose to live among the green hills;
I smile without answering, my heart at peace.
Peach blossoms float away with the stream;
There are heavens and earths beyond the world of men.

Reflections on the Moon While Drinking

WHEN did the moon first appear in the sky?
I stop drinking to pose this question.
The moon is beyond the reach of man,
Yet it follows wherever you go.
Like a bright mirror high above crimson palaces;
The green mist disperses revealing its splendour.
At night we see it rising above the ocean;
At dawn we know not where it goes among the clouds.
Year after year the white hare pounds medicine; *
Who is there to keep the lonely Chang E company?

---

* According to Chinese legend, a white hare prepares medicine with a mortar and
pestle on the moon. The goddess of the moon, Chang E, has fled there after
stealing some elixir of life from her husband.

People today cannot see the moon of ages past;
Yet the moon today has shone on our ancestors.
People pass away like a flowing stream;
Yet all have seen the moon like this.
My only wish singing and drinking wine
Is to see the moonlight in my golden goblet.

Ascending Taibai Peak[*]

ASCENDING Taibai Peak from the west,
I reach the summit in the sunset.
The morning star speaks to me,
Opening the gate of Heaven.
I wish to go with the wind,
Emerge from the floating clouds,
Raise my hand to touch the moon
And travel over all the mountains.
Once I have left Wugong,
When shall I return again?

---

[*] Taibai Peak is in Wugong, Shaanxi Province. Taibai means the morning star in Chinese. It is a fine peak in the Qinling Mountain Range.

Watching the Waterfall at Lushan

IN sunshine Censer Peak breathes purple vapour,
Far off hangs the cataract, a stream upended;
Down it cascades a sheer three thousand feet —
As if the Silver River* were falling from Heaven!

Departure from Baidicheng at Dawn**

IN the bright dawn clouds I left Baidicheng;
A thousand *li* to Jiangling*** only takes a day.
I hear the incessant cry of monkeys from the banks;
My light barge has passed countless folds of hills.

With Mother Xun at Five-Pine Hill****

AT the foot of Five-pine Hill
I stay alone, with small comfort.

---

* The Chinese name for the Milky Way.
** Baidicheng (the city of the white emperor) was situated on a hill in eastern
Sichuan.
*** Jiangling is in Hubei Province. One reaches there by travelling through the
Yangtse Gorges.
**** Near Tongling in the province of Anhui.

Farm folk toil hard in the autumn,

My neighbour husks her grain in the chill night.

Kneeling, she offers me a dish of *diao-hu*: *

Moonlight makes the white plate sparkle.

With a pang I remember the washerwoman of old; **

I thank her again and again.

But I cannot take of her food.

Drinking Alone by Moonlight

AMONG the flowers a pot of wine,

I drink alone; no friend is by.

I raise my cup, invite the moon,

And my shadow; now we are three.

But the moon knows nothing of drinking,

And my shadow only apes my doings;

Yet moon and shadow shall be my company.

Spring is the time to have fun.

I sing, the moon lingers,

I dance, my shadow tangles,

While I'm still sober, we are gay together,

When I get drunk, we go our different ways.

---

* The seed of *zizania aquatica*, which the poor used as a substitute for rice.

** At the beginning of the Han Dynasty when Han Xin, later Marquis of Huaiyin,
    was still poor and unknown, a washerwoman took pity on him and fed him.

We pledge a friendship no mortals know,

And swear to meet on heaven's Silver River.

Listening to the Lyre of a Monk Named Jun

THIS monk with his lyre came from the land of Shu*

In the west, from the high Emei Mountains.

Plucking the strings, he played for me.

I heard murmuring pines in many valleys.

Like flowing water, the music cleansed my heart,

Leaving its echo in the frosty bell.

Dusk came unnoticed to these green hills,

As the autumn clouds grew darker and darker.

---

* The land of Shu is present-day Sichuan.

Du Fu

Du Fu (712-770) was born in Gongxian County, Henan and spent the greater part of his boyhood in Luoyang. In 746 he went to Chang'an, the Tang capital, in an unsuccessful attempt to secure an official post. He fled the capital when the An Lushan rebellion broke out in 755, but was captured by the rebels. He escaped in 757 and offered his services to the new emperor. In 759 he resigned and went to Chengdu in Sichuan. He died in 770. A committed Confucian, Du Fu frequently used his poetry to expose social injustice and voice the suffering of the people. His poems include themes which hitherto would have been considered too mundane. He welcomed the newer verse forms, in particular *lü shi* or eight-line regulated verse, to which he brought his acute powers of observation and great technical skill.

The Army Carts

CARTS rumbling, horses neighing,
Men march with bows and arrows at their waists;
Parents, wives and children are there to see them off,
And Xianyang Bridge is swallowed up in dust;
Stamping and clutching the men's clothes, barring the road,
they weep;
The sound of weeping rises to the clouds.
In answer to a passer-by
The marchers say: "We're conscripts once again!
At fifteen years some here went north to guard the Yellow
River;
Now forty, we are being sent to open waste land in the
west.
When we left, the headman bound our head-cloths on;
White-haired and just home, we are off to the frontier
again!
Seas of blood have been shed at the frontier,
Yet still the emperor seeks to swell his realm.
It's said, in two hundred districts east of the Pass
Thousands of villages grow thick with brambles;
Even where sturdy women plough and hoe,
The crops are straggling in the ragged fields;
Since we of the northwest are seasoned fighters,
We are driven like dogs or hens.
You, sir, may show concern,
But how dare we soldiers complain?

Yet only this very winter
Troops west of the Pass had no rest;
The magistrate is plaguing us for taxes,
But where are taxes to come from?
We know now it is bad to bear sons,
Better to have daughters;
For a girl can be married to a next-door neighbour,
But a boy will perish like the grass in the field.
Have you not seen, beside Lake Kokonor,
Bleached bones, unburied from ancient times?
There new ghosts curse their fate and old ghosts wail;
In darkness and in rain you hear their sobbing."

Presented to Hermit Wei

IN this life friends may meet as seldom
As the stars Shen and Shang; *
Then what a rare night is this,
The two of us sharing the same candlelight!
Our youth slipped quickly by,
We are both turning grey;
Recalling old friends, now half of them ghosts,
We cry out in dismay, sick at heart.
Who could have thought that after twenty years
I should come to your house again?

---

* Orion in the west and Antares in the east.

When last we parted you were not yet married;
Suddenly, your children stand in a row before me!
Happy to welcome their father's friend,
They ask me from where I come,
And before all their questions are answered
Have brought in wine;
Spring leeks are cut in the night rain,
The freshly steamed rice has a sprinkling of yellow millet;
To mark this unlooked for encounter, my host says,
We must drain ten large cups of wine;
But today even ten cannot go to my head,
So touched by your unchanging friendship am I.
Tomorrow mountains will separate us again,
Neither knowing what the future holds.

A Lament After Travelling from the Capital to Fengxian

A homespun fellow from Duling,
More stubborn the older I grow,
What folly has made me spend my life
Trying to equal Ji and Xie* of old?
Those high hopes have come to nought
And now, white-haired, I am content with hardship;

---

* Ministers of the sage kings Yao and Shun.

But not till the lid closes on my coffin
Shall I give up my aim.
In years of want my heart yearns for the people
And, sighing, I burn with compassion;
When old schoolmates laugh at me,
Louder than ever I chant my stirring songs.
I too have dreamed of sailing far away
Free from care to watch the sun and moon revolve;
But born under a second Yao or Shun,
I cannot bear to leave my ruler's service.
True, there is no lack of good timber
To build an imperial mansion and pillars of state;
But a sunflower must look to the sun —
The nature of a thing is hard to change.
Men have I seen like ants,
Obsessed by their own nest;
But I admire the great leviathan
Resolved to rest upon the boundless deep.
From these creatures we understand life,
And since I am ashamed to seek position,
All these years poverty has been my lot,
But must I remain for ever obscure in the dust?
Not for me the hermit's life of Chao Fu and Xu You, *
Not for me to seek to change my nature;
Instead I drink deep to console myself,
And sing aloud in my sorrow.
The year is ending and the grass has withered,

---

* Two hermits in the time of the sage king Yao.

A fierce wind tears the cliffs;
Under a dark and lowering sky
I take the road at midnight
In cold so keen that when my belt falls loose
My fingers are too numb to fasten it.
At dawn I pass Li Mountain,
Where high in the crags the emperor's couch is set;
Dense mist fills the frosty air,
Valleys and cliffs are slippery underfoot,
Yet warm vapours swirl above the jade-green pool
Round which imperial guards jostle one another;
There our Prince and his court take their pleasure,
The whole vast sky rings to the sound of music,
Only the highest in the land may bathe here,
The low and wretched have no part in the feast;
But the silk shared out in the Vermilion Hall
Was woven by the hands of poor women,
Women whose men were whipped in their own homes
By tax-collectors who took the silk to the court.
The emperor makes these gifts in his infinite goodness,
In the hope that the land will prosper;
But if his ministers forget this truth,
His gifts are surely wasted!
So many courtiers now throng round the throne
That honest men must tremble;
And it's said the gold plate from the treasury
Has gone to the kinsmen of Lady Yang;
In their houses dance girls like fairies
With garments light as mist on jade-like limbs,

While the guests sit warm in sables,
And the clear lyres are followed by shrill flutes;
Rare dainties are served — the pads of camels' feet,
Winter oranges piled on fragrant tangerines;
Behind those scarlet gates meat and wine go to waste,
While out on the road lie the bones of men frozen to death;
The rich and the wretched — only a foot apart!
I cannot say more, for grief.
My carriage heads north to where two rivers meet
And at the imperial ferry turns again;
Torrents of water are tumbling down from the west,
Towering waves as far as the eye can see;
They come, surely, from the Kunlun Mountains —
Have they snapped the pillar of heaven?
Luckily the bridge still stands,
Though its joists make an ominous creaking;
And we travellers link hands to cross
This impassable waste of water.
I have left my wife far from home;
My household of ten is scattered in wind and snow;
No more must I leave them uncared for,
And so I come to share their thirst and hunger.
But wailing greets me as I cross the threshold —
Hunger has carried off my youngest boy,
And why should I try to swallow my grief
When all the neighbours are sobbing?
What sort of father have I been
To let this little one die for lack of food?
Who could foresee that after the autumn harvest

Disaster would still strike our humble home?
As for me, I am exempt from taxes,
Not named in the list of conscripts;
If such is my anguish of spirit,
How much greater the sufferings of humbler men!
When I think of those with no work
Or sent to garrison the distant frontiers,
My sorrow rises high as Zhongnan Mountain,
Too great to be swept aside.

Lament on the Defeat at Chentao

Early winter, and the best of our youth from ten provinces
Has turned to blood the water of the Chentao marshes; *
Wide the plain and clear the sky, with no noise of battle,
For all in one day forty thousand good men gave their lives.
The Tartars returned to wash the blood from their arrows,
To sing Tartar songs as they drink in the marketplace;
But we in Chang'an turn our faces north and weep,
Waiting day and night for the government troops' return.

---

* In the tenth month of 756, Emperor Suzong tried to recapture Luoyang and
Chang'an, but the Tang forces were routed at Chentao, and more than forty
thousand men perished. Du Fu was in Chang'an at the time of the defeat.

Sorrow at the End of the Canal

A peasant from Shaoling suppresses a sob, *
Wandering quietly in spring by the canal. **
All the palace's thousand gates are locked;
Who enjoys the green willows and rushes?
He recalls the emperor's gay banners,
Which increased the splendour of the south park.
There was the first lady of the Zhaoyang Palace***
Who rode with the emperor in the same carriage.
Before went a maid with bow and arrows,
Upon a white steed with a golden bit and bridle.
Leaning back, she shot an arrow at the clouds;
A bird fell, and the lady smiled.
Where is this beauty with bright eyes and teeth?
Her blood-stained, restless ghost shall never return.
The clear Wei River flows east; the Sword Pass is distant. ****
No communication between the living and the dead.
People with feeling must shed tears.
Water flows on, and blossoms fade.

---

* Shaoling was Du Fu's ancestral district.
** The canal referred to was the Qujiang Canal, situated in southeast Chang'an.
*** Zhaoyang Palace was the palace of the Empress Zhao Feiyan in the Han Dynasty. The first lady referred to here was Lady Yang, the favourite of the Emperor Xuanzong.
**** In 765, An Lushan revolted and captured the capital. The emperor fled to Sichuan. On the way at Mawei Station, the guards mutinied and demanded the death of Lady Yang. The emperor was forced to sacrifice her. The Wei River was near the spot where she was killed. The Sword Pass was where the emperor passed on his way to Sichuan.

At dusk as the Huns return, dust rises over the city.
Wanting to go south, he still looks north.

Thoughts

SINCE the loss of Tongguan to the rebels last year,
I've long been parted from my wife and children.
This summer as the grass and trees grew,
I freed myself and went westwards.
Still in my hempen sandals I met the emperor;
My sleeves were worn, my elbows exposed.
Officials praised me for my safe return;
Relatives and friends were sad to see I'd aged.
With tears of gratitude I took an adviser's post,
My emperor's benevolence in my distress.
Although I could return to my country home,
I could not immediately mention my desire.
I wrote a letter to send to Sanchuan,
Wondering if my home still existed.
Then I heard that district had been razed;
Even chickens and dogs had been slaughtered.
Who would be waiting at the door
Of my dilapidated, thatched, mountain hut?
The old pine is crushed at the root;
The ground is cold with rotting corpses.
How many have escaped with their lives?
How many families remain intact?

Sick at heart I look back
To the mountain village which the tigers ravaged.
Since the day I sent my letter,
Ten months have passed already.
I dread to receive news from home;
What hope can lie within my heart?
This is the time to revive our dynasty,
As I grow old and fond of wine.
When I think of our happy reunion,
I fear to end my days alone and poor.

Fleeing Through Pengya

I recall when I first fled the rebels,
Northwards through dangers and difficulties,
Late at night trudging through Pengya,
The moon shone on the Baishui Mountains.
Long had my family gone on foot,
Unashamed to meet a stranger.
Occasionally hearing only the sound of birds,
Seldom seeing a traveller returning.
Crazed with hunger my daughter bit me, crying,
While I feared a tiger or wolf might hear.
Stopping her mouth I carried her in my arms,
While she struggled, howling even more.
My son, thinking he was clever,
Demanded bitter, wild berries to eat.

Thunderstorms for half the ten days;
We dragged each other through the mud.
With no protection against the rain,
The path slippery, our bodies cold.
Sometimes the way seemed impassable,
In one day we covered only a few *li*.
We fed on wild fruits,
Low branches were our roof.
Mornings we waded through water, stepping on stones;
Evenings we rested on the misty heights.
Briefly we paused at Tongjiawa,
Considering going by the Luzi Pass.
There I found an old friend, Sun Zai,
Whose sense of friendship reached the clouds.
It was night when he invited me home,
Taking his lamp, unbarring his door.
Then he brought hot water to wash my feet,
And cut paper charms to invoke my spirit.
Summoning forth his wife and children,
We looked at each other shedding tears,
My children were fast asleep;
So I awoke them and ate together.
He vowed to always be my sworn brother;
Then left his sitting-room
For our comfort and ease.
Who else would be so generous, opening his heart
At a time when I was in such a sorry plight?
A year has passed since our parting;
The Tartar rebels are still making trouble.

If only I had wings
To fly and see you again.

Dreaming of Li Bai

WERE we parted by death, I might swallow my grief,
But to be parted in life is pain unending;
South of the Yangtse is a malarial region,
And still no news of the exile;
Yet you appear, my old friend, in my dreams,
Which shows how you fill my thoughts.
But was this the spirit of a living man?
So far away, there is no way of knowing!
Through the green maple forest you came,
Returning by dark passes and fortresses.
Caught in a net,
How did you take wings to fly?
When the dying moon lights the rafters of my room
I can almost see your face reflected there.
Deep the river, wild the waves;
Beware of dragons and serpents!

All day the clouds drift by;
Too long has the wanderer been away.
These three nights I have dreamed of you
And seen the love in your heart;
But every time you took a hasty leave,

For the way was rough, the journey hard,
Many the storms on rivers and on lakes
And easy for a small boat to capsize;
So off you went, rubbing your hoary head,
Like one who has failed in a lifelong ambition.
Officials in all their state throng the capital,
You alone are careworn, passed over.
Who speaks of justice when Heaven casts its net?
My friend in his old age is caught in the toils.
His name will live for centuries to come,
But fame is little comfort after death.

Phoenix Tower

SHEER rises Phoenix Tower,
Overlooking Xikang to the north;
But now the Lord of the West* is no more,
The phoenix, too, is hushed.
Steep and trackless the mountain
And rarefied the air in that forest of crags;
Would I had a ladder reaching to the clouds
To climb the heights for you!
Perhaps some fledgeling phoenix without a mother
Is chirping there day after day, hungry and cold;

---

* King Wen, first king of the Zhou Dynasty in the eleventh century B. C. The
Lord of the West was his title before he became king. According to the legend,
the crying of a phoenix was heard in Qi Mountain where he lived.

And I could give my life's blood
To sustain the sad, lonely bird.
My heart would serve instead of bamboo-seeds,
For my heart is honest and free from other desires;
My blood would serve instead of sweet spring water.
For I strive for more than my own integrity,
Setting such store by this kingly, auspicious portent
That for it I would gladly lay down my life.
Let me sit and watch the bird's bright plumage grow,
Till it soars freely round the universe,
Fetching from heaven an auspicious plan
And flying down from the twelve jade pavilions;
The noble plan will be offered to the emperor,
And the phoenix will bring it to pass;
Once more the empire will prosper,
Grief and care will be swept away.
This, above all, is my deepest concern —
That rebels may vanish from the land.

White Sand Ferry

FEARFUL that way by the far-stretching river,
Where the steep bank dips down to the ferry;
Junks are straggling upstream
To be lost, far off, in the clouds;
Cold is the sky beyond this rugged landscape,
And the end of day finds us mid-stream;

My horse turns to the north and neighs,
Monkeys chatter to each other as they drink;
Clear runs the water, craggy loom the rocks,
White is the sand, endless the winding shore;
Far from the world I shed my griefs and cares
And find some ease in my infirmity.
I come to the foot of these towering cliffs
To cross where the torrent surges in wilder fury;
Alone, the wind on my face, I turn my head
And reining in my horse heave heavy sighs.

My Thatched Hut Is Wrecked by
the Autumn Wind

THE eighth month and a mid-autumn gale
Tore off the three layers of my thatch;
Across the stream flew the straw to scatter the banks,
Caught high up on tall trees
Or fluttering down into the pools and ditches.
The village boys found a feeble old man easy game,
And robbed me to my face,
Openly lugging off armfuls through the bamboos,
Though I shouted till I was hoarse and my lips parched.
I went home then, leaning on my stick, and sighed.
Soon the wind fell and black clouds gathered,
The autumn sky grew dark as dusk came on;

My quilt after years of use is cold as iron,
With rents kicked in it by my spoiled, restless son;
The roof, no patch of it dry, leaks over my bed
And the rain streams through like unending strands of
    hemp;
Ever since the rebellion I have been losing sleep;
Wet through, how can I last out this long night till dawn?

Oh, for a great mansion with ten thousand rooms
Where all the poor on earth could find welcome shelter,
Steady through every storm, secure as a mountain!
Ah, were such a building to spring up before me,
I would freeze to death in my wrecked hut well content.

On Women Selling Firewood

KUIZHOU* women remain single till middle age,
Their hair already turning grey.
In time of wars and death, marriage is more difficult;
So they sigh and regret their lives.
By custom the man sits while the woman stands;
He is master of the house; she the servant.
Most women bring firewood home to sell
While officials take the money as levies.
They age with their girlish tresses at their necks,

---

* Kuizhou is in eastern Sichuan Province.

Wild flowers and leaves caught in a silver clasp.
Their bodies ache from the perilous climb to the fairs;
Tears smear the powder on their faces,
They risk death to sell illegal salt for profit. *
Thinly clad they struggle below the narrow rocks.
If you say such women are coarse and plain,
Why was a village named after Wang Zhaojun?**

Hearing Piping at Night

AT night I hear piping on the river,
And bend my old ears towards those stirring notes;
These strains from a neighbouring boat fill my heart with
    grief,
This air from the border has heightened pathos at midnight;
A bitter night is this of frost and snowdrifts,
Yet the piping shrills through the storm to my lonely lamp.
Yes, friend, when the clash of arms fills all the earth,
Hard the journeying across rivers and lakes.

---

 * Salt wells were located near Kuizhou, but were a government monopoly. People
   selling salt illegally could be severely punished.
** Wang Zhaojun was a well-known beauty in the Han Dynasty. Her native village
   was near Kuizhou.

One Moonlight Night

ON this moonlight night in Fuzhou
She will be watching in her room alone;
Far away, my heart aches for our children,
Too young to remember Chang'an. *
Her cloudy hair will be damp in the fragrant mist,
Her jade-white arms cold in the limpid light;
When shall we lean together by gauze curtains,
Side by side beneath the moon, all our tears dried?

Thinking of My Brothers in the Moonlight

THE drum from the watchtower sounds; all are forbidden to
    move.
In autumn in this frontier town, a lone swan is heard.
This is the season when the dew turns white, **
But the moon seems brighter at my home.
I have brothers but all are scattered.
Homeless now, I know not if they're alive or dead.
The letters I have written never reach them,
Especially now that war is raging.

---

* Du Fu was in the capital, which had been captured by the rebels.
** According to the Chinese calendar there are twenty-four festivals each year. The
White Dew Festival falls about 8th September.

Welcome Rain One Spring Night

A good rain knows its season
And comes when spring is here;
On the heels of the wind it slips secretly into the night,
Silent and soft, it moistens everything.
Now clouds hang black above the country roads,
A lone boat on the river sheds a glimmer of light;
At dawn we shall see splashes of rain-washed red —
Drenched, heavy blooms in the City of Brocade. *

Taking Pleasure by the Balustrade
over the Water

FAR from town this pavilion with the sweeping prospect,
And no villages to block the distant view;
The clear stream flows peacefully between low banks,
The quiet trees in the dusk are a mass of blooms;
Light rain brings small fish to the surface,
A soft breeze makes the swallows heel over;
The city has a hundred thousand households,
Here, two or three families only.

---

* Another name for Chengdu.

Hearing of the Recovery of the Regions North and South of the River by the Imperial Forces

THROUGH the Sword Pass comes sudden news of recovered
    lands in the north,
And, hearing it, I drench my clothes with tears.
I gaze at my wife and children, all grief forgotten,
And roll up my papers at random, wild with joy.
The sun has not set, yet I feel I must drink and sing;
Lovely spring shall be our companion as home we go;
We shall sail through the Yangtse Gorges
Down to Xiangyang and the road to old Luoyang!

Climbing a Terrace

WIND blusters high in the sky and monkeys wail;
Clear the islet with white sand where birds are wheeling;
Everywhere the leaves fall rustling from the trees,
While on for ever rolls the turbulent Yangtse.
All around is autumnal gloom and I, long from home,
A prey all my life to ill health, climb the terrace alone;
Hating the hardships which have frosted my hair,
Sad that illness has made me give up the solace of wine.

Thoughts When Travelling at Night

BETWEEN soft, grassy banks in the light breeze
A lone, tall-masted boat sails through the night;
Stars hang low above the wide, flat plain,
And up rides the moon as the mighty river flows on.
Since I have not in truth won fame by writing,
In old age and illness I should retire from office.
Drifting along, to what can I liken myself?
A lonely beach gull between heaven and earth.

The White Emperor's City

FROM the White Emperor's City clouds are drifting;
Below, rain pours down like a basin overturned;
Flood waters rush through the gorge, thunder battles with
    lightning;
Sun and moon grow dim among green trees and grey vines.
War-horses are not as content as horses at grass,
Of a thousand families only a hundred are left;
Widows ruined by cruel taxation are in despair,
Sobbing sounds on the autumn plain in every village.

Climbing the Yueyang Tower

I have long heard of Lake Dongting;
Now I ascend the Yueyang Tower. *
It separates the lands of Wu and Chu,**
One in the east, the other in the south.
The sun and moon seem to float there day and night.
I have heard nothing from my family and friends;
Growing old and ill, alone I sail in a barge.
War rages in the northern mountain passes;
Leaning on a balustrade I shed tears.

---

* The Yueyang Tower was the west gate-tower of Yueyang city. Lake Dongting
was close beside it.
** The Kingdom of Wu was in the east, in present-day Jiangsu Province. The Kingdom of Chu was in the southwest, in present-day Hubei and Hunan.

HAN YU

Han Yu (768-824), from Mengxian County in Henan, was considered by many to be the finest writer of classical prose after Sima Qian. He was the leader of the *gu wen* or "old prose" movement which opposed the formal and contrived style of the day, and advocated the use of clearer language and simpler and more colloquial diction and syntax. Although he is most famous as an essayist and polemicist in defence of Confucianism, Han Yu was also a writer of fresh and original verse. His writing has exerted a considerable influence on later generations.

A Painting

A small scroll of people and things, ancient and modern.

Five horsemen; ten armed horsemen bearing weapons; a horseman at their head with a large standard; ten armed horsemen bearing weapons, moving away, some of them leading their mounts; two horsemen carrying loads; two carrying utensils; one with a hound; two pulling on the reins; three horsemen galloping; two men standing and holding the halter and reins; one horseman with a hawk on his arm, leaning against his steed; two horsemen galloping across a stream; two shepherds on foot; one seated man giving orders; seven men erect in armour and helmets, holding bows, arrows and axes; ten men in armour and helmets standing with flags; seven men carrying loads; two lying down to rest; one in armour and helmet dozing on foot; one fording a stream; one sitting down and taking off his boots; one warming himself by the fire; eight serving-men with utensils; one man with a cottabus; eleven men camping and preparing food; four men pouring drinks; two pulling oxen; four riding donkeys; one man with a stick carrying a load; six women with children in carriages; three women getting down from or into carriages; nine children playing. In all there are thirty-two different actions, and one hundred and twenty-three people, each different from the rest.

Among the horses are nine large ones. Some are at the top of the scroll, some at the bottom. They are moving away, being led, fording the stream, jumping, raising their hooves, looking back, neighing, sleeping, waking, standing, rearing, champing, drinking, urinating, climbing up or down, rubbing against trees, panting, snuffling, frisking, kicking, biting, being fed, being ridden, galloping, cantering, carrying utensils or dead foxes and rabbits. There are twenty-seven different actions and eighty-three horses, each different from the rest.

There are eleven large and small oxen, three camels, one more donkey than there are camels, one hawk, thirty dogs, sheep, foxes, rabbits and stags. There are three carriages, and two hundred and fifty-one pieces of equipment, including bows and arrows, flags, swords, lances, shields, quivers sheaths, suits of armour and helmets. There are jugs, bowls and other utensils for eating and drinking, as well as umbrellas, straw hats, baskets and pots. There are also games like cottabus and draughts. All are exquisitely drawn.

In the cyclic year of Jiaxu* during the Zhenyuan era, I was in the capital with time on my hands. My fellow lodger, Dugu Shenshu, had acquired this painting, but I was lucky enough to beat him at shovelboard and win it as my prize. I was enchanted by it, and doubted whether it could have been conceived by one painter, for it had the merits of many. I would not have parted with it for a hundred gold pieces.

The next year I left the capital and went to Heyang. During a discussion with a few friends about the merits of different paintings, I showed them this. Among those present was Censor Zhao, a true gentleman, who looked distressed and moved when he saw this scroll. Later he came to me and confessed with a sigh:

* A.D. 794.

"That is a copy I made, which I lost nearly twenty years ago. When I was young, I was interested in painting. I found a scroll by a great master, and made the very best copy I could of it; but in Minzhou I lost it. In my spare moments I often remember it, for I worked so hard to copy it and was so fond of it. But now that I have found it again, it is beyond my powers. I would like to get a painter to make me a rough sketch of it."

Attached as I was to this painting, I was so touched by Censor Zhao's story that I presented it to him, having first listed the position and number of the people and objects in it to read from time to time, to console myself for my loss.

Wang Chengfu, the Plasterer

A plasterer's trade is humble and hard, yet I know one who appears content with his lot. His talk is to the point and covers the subject. When asked, he told me his name was Wang Chengfu.

"My folk were peasants outside Chang'an for generations," he said. "In the rebellion during the Tianbao era, when men were conscripted for the army, I served as an archer for thirteen years and was given official awards. Then I gave that up and went home. As my land had gone, I made a living with my trowel. For the last thirty years I have rented a room in the market, and to pay for my board and lodging I see what prices are at the time and charge more or less for my labour. Whatever is left over I give to the maimed, the sick and the starving in the streets."

"Grain is grown by the farmers," he went on. "To make cloth

or silk you must rear silkworms and weave. Our daily needs are supplied by the work of men's hands, and I need all these things. But as no man can follow every trade, each must do his part to help his fellows. The ruler orders the means by which we live, and his officers spread his influence. Some tasks are big, some small, and each does what he can like vessels of different sizes. If a man takes pay but slacks on his job, he must come to a bad end. That is why I have not dared leave my trowel for one day to have a little fun. Working with a trowel is easy and within my power, and the service is useful; so I am not ashamed to take payment for it, and my heart is at peace. It is easy to get results by using your brawn, but hard to increase your knowledge by using your brain — that is why it is right for workers by hand to serve and for workers by brain to rule. I have picked an easy job and one I have no cause to be ashamed of. Yet, I have gone for years now with my trowel to the homes of the rich and great. Maybe the second time the house is in ruins, maybe the third or fourth time. When I ask the neighbours what has happened they say: 'Oh, they were executed.' 'The master died and his heirs could not keep it up.' Or, 'After they died their property was confiscated.' As I see it, these are all cases of men who take pay but slack on the job and bring trouble on their own heads. They try to be clever without the brain for it, and take something on without stopping to think whether they are up to it or not. They behave disgracefully, and insist on doing what they know is wrong. Riches and rank cannot last when slight achievements go with great self-indulgence. Wealth is followed by want and cannot last for ever. Because I pity such cases, I do what I am fit for. It is not that I am different from other folk who like riches and rank and hate poverty and low position."

"Those with great achievements to their credit can keep themselves in luxury," he went on. "A man with a wife and children has to support them, and as I am not up to much and have not much to my credit either, I may as well do without them. I am a manual labourer. If I had a family and could not keep it, that would prey on my mind too, and not even a sage could stand the double strain."

At first I was sceptical, but on second thoughts I decided he was a wise man, one of those who are content to look after themselves well. Yet I have some criticism too. Do those who do too much for themselves and not enough for others subscribe to Yang Zhu's* philosophy? According to Yang Zhu, a man should not pull out one hair of his head to benefit the world. This plasterer believes that to have a family would mean exercising his mind over his wife and children, and he refuses to do anything for others. Still, he is much better than those who worry about not having enough or losing something they have, men with wicked appetites who forget the Way and destroy themselves in the end. Indeed his words hold a warning for me. I set this down, then, as a mirror for myself.

---

* A philosopher of the Warring States period (403-221 B.C.).

Reply to Li Yi's Letter

ON the twenty-sixth day of the sixth month, Han Yu sends Li Yi greetings. Your letter, sir, is most excellently written, yet your request is so modest and respectful, how could the one to whom it is addressed not be glad to answer it?

The Truth has long since departed, much more so the literature which was its outward form. Though I am one who can be said to have caught a glimpse of the gate and wall of the Sage's mansion, I have not yet entered the hall and am therefore unable to distinguish between right and wrong; yet I feel constrained to speak of it to you, sir.

Your desire to make your mark by writing is good, and what you have done comes very close to your aim; but I do not know whether your ambition is to learn from contemporaries and try to surpass them, or to aspire to reach the standard of the ancients. If the former is the case, you are sure to succeed; but you cannot expect quick results if you want to reach the standard of the ancients, nor must you be obsessed with the desire for gain. You should nurture the root but not hasten the fruit, add nutriment but not strive for lustre. When the root is vigorous, the tree will be laden with fruit; when the nutriment is rich, the lustre will shine; the writing of a humane and just man should be mild.

However, this is difficult and I do not know whether I have achieved it or not, although this has been my study for twenty years and more. In the beginning, I dared not read any books but those of the Han Dynasty and earlier ages, nor dared I harbour any ideas apart from those of the sages. Remaining in one place,

I seemed to forget where I was; going out, I seemed to have mislaid something. I looked solemn as if deep in thought, dazed as if I had lost my way. When I tried to set down what was in my mind, I wanted to rid myself of all stereotyped phrases, but I found this an arduous task. When others read my writing I would not know whether they were laughing at me.

After some years spent undeflectingly in this way, what was true or false in ancient books, or what was correct but not completely so, became as clear to me as black and white, and I began to learn how to discard what was wrong. When now I tried to set down what was in my mind, the ideas flowed freely. When I saw people laughing at me, I felt pleased; what worried me was when they praised me, for that meant there were still other people's views in my writing.

After some more years spent like this, I was like a river in spate. But for fear of confusion, I confronted my writing and checked it soberly. Finding it pure enough, I cast off restraint.

Nevertheless, I have to go on cultivating myself, keeping to the path of humanity and justice and going to the source of the ancient classics. I must never till the end of my days lose my way or forget the source.

The spirit is the water, language what floats upon it. When water abounds, all objects large and small can float upon it. So it is with the spirit and language: when the spirit abounds, all writing whether long or short, high-toned or low, will be appropriate.

Even so, can I be of any use to people? However, literature that expects to be of use is like a utensil: whether it is used or rejected depends on others. A noble-minded man is different: he

has the Truth in his heart and his conduct is principled; if used,
he will benefit others; if rejected, he will pass on his teachings to
his disciples and hand down his writings as models for future generations.

Is this sufficient cause for gratification? Very few now aspire
to reach the standard of the ancients. Those who do will be forsaken by the present age. So I feel both pleased and sad for such
men and can only encourage them, not venturing either to praise
or censure them. Many people have consulted me, but judging by
what you say, sir, your aim is not profit, and so I have spoken of
this. Here ends my letter.

A Farewell to Li Yuan

SOUTH of the Taihang Mountains is Meander Vale. Its springs
are sweet, its soil fruitful, and few men live in its well-wooded
groves. Some say it is called Meander because the valley winds
around to mountains. Others say that, secluded and difficult of
access, it is a place where hermits love to wander. Here my
friend Li Yuan dwells.

Li Yuan once said: "I know what is commonly meant by a
great man — one who renders service to the people, whose fame
adds lustre to his age, who has a seat at court, appoints and recalls officials, and assists the emperor in issuing edicts. If he
serves in the provinces, flags are set up and bows and arrows dis-
played, guards before him raise a shout, his followers block the
way, and attendants bearing objects for his use gallop down both

sides of the road. When pleased, he gives rewards; when angry, he metes out punishments. He is surrounded by men of outstanding talent, who talk of past and present and praise his virtue, and whose speech is pleasing and gives no offence. Room after room of dainty, clear-voiced girls with arched eyebrows and plump cheeks, lovely and witty in light, longsleeved gowns, wait idly with powdered faces and darkened eyebrows, jealous of his favourite and eager to charm him. This is the life of a great man who is recognized by the emperor and can make his influence felt in the government. I am not opposed to this or anxious to avoid such a position, but it depends on fate, not on any turn of fortune."

"A poor man whose time is his own may climb a hill to gaze into the distance, sit in the shade of a fine tree all day, bathe in clear springs, pick sweet herbs on the mountain, or catch fresh fish in the pools. He gets up or lies down as the fancy takes him, prefers a blameless end to fame at the start, and an untroubled mind to physical pleasures. He receives no imperial honours and no harsh punishment either; he does not know whether times are good or bad, or which men have been degraded or promoted. This is the way of a great man who has not won recognition, and this is how I live."

"Others may wait at the gates of ministers, hurry in pursuit of the mighty, hesitate before each step, stammer in their speech, and feel no shame at their own degradation. They incur punishments or are executed, staking all on a single toss till they die of old age. My way is infinitely superior."

I, Han Yu of Changli, heard and approved this speech. I offered him wine and sang this song to him:

Meander Valley is your home,
Meander's soil you till;
Beside Meander's springs you roam,
And yours is every hill.
Meander is secure and blessed,
A quiet, hushed domain,
Whose mountains with their sloping sides
Wind round and back again.
No savage tigers dare come near,
And there no serpents coil,
For kindly spirits watch above
To guard its happy soil.
Then eat and drink and take your ease;
May all your dreams come true!
I'll wax my carriage, groom my steeds,
And seek Meander too,
To ramble in Meander Vale
With you my whole life through.

A Letter to Cui Qun

SINCE you left the eastern capital, you have done me the honour
of writing to me twice. I understand that you have reached Xuanzhou, that your host is a humane and excellent man and your
colleagues true gentlemen; so though conscious that you are far
from home, you are doing fairly well there. A man should be

able to find happiness anywhere, provided he accepts the will of
Heaven cheerfully. This is how good men in the past dealt with
circumstances, and you who are so much superior to all others
will certainly not allow your spirit to be fettered by minor consid-
erations. Though Xuanzhou is said to be cool and high, no place
south of the Yangtse can compare with the climate of the north.
For the sake of your health you should first regulate your
thoughts, for once your heart is at ease no extraneous evils will
be able to touch you, you will know how to adapt yourself, and
will not suffer from any indisposition. If a man of your worth
can remain happy even in a poor position, how should they feel
who serve near the court, hold a highly paid office, and have all
their dear ones beside them! I am dwelling on this because I consider a man of your calibre ought to fill an important position,
and a secretary's post is unworthy of you. I speak out of love and
respect, not that I imagine you need advice of this sort.

Since my boyhood I have spent seventeen years among acquain-
tances and friends. This is not a short time, and my associates
number about a thousand — no small figure — including quite a
few who have been as close to me as brothers. Some worked with
me, others shared my interests, had gifts which I admired or
were friends of long standing. With some I was not too intimate
to begin with, but as we grew better acquainted and I found they
had no great faults I kept up the friendship. Yet others were not
entirely good, but they treated me so well that I could not break
with them. I am speaking here of close friends, not casual ac-
quaintances. You are the only man, though, before whom I am
prostrated in admiration, in whose words and actions I can find
no flaw, whose measure I cannot take, whose character is bril-

liant and unsullied, and whose greatness becomes daily more apparent. Dull though I am and lacking in understanding, I have read all the sages' books. I may not have mastered them in their entirety with all their subtleties and shades of meaning, but I have at least dipped into them. And certainly, in my judgment and estimation, you stand head and shoulders above your contemporaries — there is no gainsaying this. Between friends like ourselves, such explanations are needless. I have said this for fear you may think the number of my intimates shows a lack of discrimination. It is also wrong, of course, to claim to understand you more or less and yet be afraid that you misunderstand me. A friend of mine once said that while he agreed you were nearly perfect, he still had certain reservations. I asked him the reason.

"A gentleman should have his likes and dislikes, and must make them clear," he said. "Yet wise men and fools alike praise Cui's good qualities and look up to him. That is why I have reservations."

"Wise men and fools alike consider the phoenix and the herb of immortality auspicious," said I. "Even slaves know that the brilliant sun and blue sky are clear and bright. It is the same with food — rare dishes from distant lands are appreciated by some and not by others, but one and all like rice and millet, and meat whether minced or cooked."

So I convinced the man. But whether others doubt you or not cannot detract from your greatness.

From ancient times there have been few men of talent but many mediocrities. Since I reached the age of discretion, I have seen many talented men meet with ill fortune while mediocrities received official honours. I have seen talented men unable to earn a living while mediocrities grew proud and mighty. I have seen talented men die young after holding some low position, while mediocrities lived to a ripe old age. I do not understand the Creator's plan. Can it be that he has different views from men? Or is he so forgetful that he does not care whether mortals live or perish, die in old age or in youth? There is no knowing. Some there are who despise the post of a minister and a fief of a thousand chariots, content with vegetable broth in a narrow lane. Since even human beings have such different standards, Heaven must differ even more. And there can be no harm in something which accords with Heaven's way but not with the way of men, much less with that which happens to accord with both. Take heart, then, Mr Cui!

I have no adequate means of support, but have grown poorer and poorer since taking up my post here. I should like to go and live by the banks of the Yi or the Ying, and I dare say I shall manage this eventually. Recently I have aged even more. My second molar tooth on the left grew loose and has come out for no apparent reason. My eyes are now so dim that I cannot distinguish faces at ten or twenty feet. Half the hair on my temples is white, as well as one-fifth on my head and even one or two of the hairs in my beard. My family is unlucky. As my uncles and elder brothers died young although their health was good, I can hardly hope to live to a great age. This depresses me, and I long to see you again to talk of everything that is in my heart. The sight of my children cannot but make me anxious. When will you be able to return north? I do not enjoy the south, and as soon as I have completed my term of office I mean to retire to the foot of the Song Mountains. You might join me there — I shall not be leaving again. Look after your health, be careful what you eat and drink, and do not worry too much I beg of you. I send respectful greetings.

A Farewell to Meng Jiao

MOST things when not at peace will sound. Plants and trees have no voice, but rustled by the wind they sound. Water has no voice, but ruffled by the wind it sounds, splashing when struck, gathering speed when obstructed, and seething when heated. Metal and stone have no voice, but when beaten they sound. And human utterances are the same: men speak out when forced to it. If they long for something, they sing; if they are sad, they weep. Sounds pass their lips whenever they are not at peace.

Music expresses what has been pent up, and chooses the most resonant substances for its sounds. Metal, stone, strings, bamboo, gourds, earthenware, leather and wood — these eight have resonance. It is the same with the seasons of the year: they choose the most resonant things to transmit sound. Thus birds warble in spring, thunder rumbles in summer, crickets chirp in autumn, and the wind howls in winter; for while the four seasons rotate there cannot be peace.

It is the same with men. Language is the essence of human speech, literature the essence of language, and the most articulate are chosen as spokesmen. In the time of the sage kings Yao and Shun, Gao Yao and Yu were chosen as spokesmen for they were the most articulate, while Kuei spoke through the Shao dance since he could not express himself through literature. In the Xia Dynasty the five brothers spoke through their song. Yi Yin was the voice of the Shang Dynasty, and the Duke of Zhou of the Zhou Dynasty. The *Book of Songs*, the *Book of History* and the other classics are the best voice of that time. When the house of Zhou declined, the followers of Confucius spoke out with a mighty voice which carried far and wide. True, indeed, was the saying: "Heaven will use the master as a tocsin." Towards the end of that period, Zhuang Zi spoke through his allegories. When the great kingdom of Chu fell, Qu Yuan spoke. Zang Wenzhong, Mencius and Xun Zi spoke through their different doctrines. Men like Yang Zhu, Mo Di, Guan Zhong, Yan Ying, Lao Dan, Shen Buhai, Han Fei, Shen Dao, Tian Pian, Zou Yan, Shi Jiao, Sun Wu, Zhang Yi and Su Qin spoke through their art. In the Qin Dynasty's heyday, Li Si's voice was heard. Sima Qian, Sima Xiangru and Yang Xiong were the best voice of the Han Dynasty. The spokesmen of the Wei and Jin dynasties were not the equal of the men of old, but there was never silence. The best literature of this period was light and clear in tone, swift and impetuous in rhythm, sentimental and extravagant in language, reckless and abandoned in spirit; and the ideas it expressed were confused and undeveloped. Was this because Heaven had condemned the age and was not watching over it? And if not, why were there no better singers?

When the Tang Dynasty was founded, Chen Zi'ang, Su Yuanming, Yuan Jie, Li Bai, Du Fu and Li Guan all sang in their different ways. Since their time Meng Jiao has started to sing with his poems which surpass those of the Wei and Jin dynasties and are worthy of the men of old, while others approach the Han poets. Of these my friends Li Ao and Zhang Jie are the best. The songs of these three men are undoubtedly fine. But does Heaven intend them to sing in harmony of the empire's prosperity, or, hungry and poor, weighed down by cares, to sing of their misfortunes? It is Heaven which decides the fate of mortal men. One may not be happy in a high position, or distressed in a humble one.

Now Meng Jiao is being sent to work in the south, and seems reluctant to go. It is to comfort him that I point out that men's fate is determined by Heaven.

On Teachers

SINCE ancient times to learn all men must have teachers, who pass on the truth and dispel ignorance. As men are not born wise, who can be free from ignorance? But if ignorant men do not find teachers, they remain ignorant for ever. Some teachers may be born before me and have learned the truth before me; I should therefore learn from them. Some may have been born after me, but learned the truth before me; I should also learn from them. As I seek the truth, I need not worry whether my teacher is my senior or junior. Whether he is noble or common, elder or younger, whoever knows the truth can be a teacher.

Alas, since men have long ceased learning from teachers it is hard not to be ignorant. The old sages were far superior to common men, yet they sought the truth from teachers. Most men of today are far below those sages, yet they think it shameful to learn. That is why sages become more sage, while fools become more foolish. No doubt this is what makes some sages and others fools.

A man who loves his son chooses a teacher for him but is ashamed to find one for himself. This is entirely wrong. All a child's teacher can do is give him a book and tell him how to read it sentence by sentence. This is not the teacher I have in mind who can pass on the truth and dispel ignorance. If we want to learn to read not to dispel ignorance, we are learning the lesser and giving up the greater, which is hardly intelligent.

Physicians, musicians and artisans are not ashamed to learn from each other. But if one of the literati calls another man his teacher and himself the pupil, people will flock to laugh at him. If you ask why, they will reply that the men are roughly equal in age and understanding. If one has a low social status, it is humiliating; if one is a high official, it looks like flattery. Clearly, to learn from a teacher is old-fashioned. Physicians, musicians and artisans are despised by gentlemen, yet they seem to be more intelligent. Is this not strange?

A sage has more than one teacher. Thus Confucius learned from Tan Zi, Chang Hong, Shi Xiang and Lao Dan. Men like Tan Zi were inferior to Confucius, yet Confucius said: "Out of three men, there must be one who can teach me." So pupils are not necessarily inferior to their teachers, nor teachers better than their pupils. Some learn the truth earlier than others, and some have special skills — that is all.

Li Pan is seventeen. He is fond of ancient literature, and has studied the six arts, the classics and the commentaries, not confining himself to what is in vogue today. He has studied with me, and as I admire his respect for the old traditions I am writing this essay on teachers for him.

In Memory of My Nephew

SEVEN days after I, your uncle, heard of your death, with heart-felt grief in this distant place I made Jianzhong prepare offerings of the season to sacrifice to your spirit.

Alas! Left an orphan early, I grew up with no recollection of my father, brought up by my elder brother and his wife — your parents. When my brother was cut off in his prime in the south, you and I, still boys, went with your mother to Heyang for the funeral, and later found a livelihood south of the Yangtse. Two lonely, fatherless lads, we were never parted for a single day.

My three elder brothers died young, leaving you as the only grandson and me as the only son to carry on our line — each the sole representative of his generation. Your mother used to pat you and point at me, saying: "You two are all that are left of two generations of the house of Han." You were too young to have remembered, and I, though old enough to remember her words, did not know the grief behind them.

At nineteen I went to the capital. Four years later I returned to you, and in four more years, when I visited our ancestral graves at Heyang, I found you burying your mother there. Two years later you came to stay with me for a year while I was working with Minister Dong at Bianzhou, and then you went home to fetch your family. Next year the minister died, I left Bianzhou, and you were unable to join me. That year I was appointed to assist the governor of Xuzhou, but no sooner did I send for you than I had to leave again, so that once more you could not join me. I feared if you were to go with me to the east, where you too were a stranger, we could not stay there long. My best plan for the future was to return west, and fetch you after settling my household there.

Alas, who could have foreseen that you would so soon leave me and die? As we were both still young, I thought that after a temporary separation we would pass the long evening of our life together. That is why I left you to find a post in the capital, for the sake of a few bushels of government rice. Had I known that this would happen, I would not have parted with you for a single day, not for a dukedom or a ministership with a fief of ten thousand chariots.

Last year when Meng Jiao left, I wrote to you: "I am not yet forty, yet my sight is failing, my hair is greying, my teeth are giving me trouble. Considering how early my uncles and brothers died, though all of them were strong men, how long can a crock like myself hope to last? I cannot leave my post, and you will not come. But if I were to die suddenly, you would be sorry ever after."

To think that the younger would die and the elder live on! That the stronger would go, not the invalided! Alas! Is this reality or a dream? Perhaps the news is not true. If it is, how could the heir of a man as noble as my brother be struck down? How could one of your integrity not survive to carry on his line? Are the young and strong cut off, while the old and weak live on? I cannot believe it. But if this is a dream and the news not true, why are Meng's letter and Geng Lan's report before me? Alas, it is true after all! My noble brother's heir has indeed died before his time! Despite your integrity and fitness to head the family, you did not survive to carry on his line! These untimely deaths are unpredictable, Heaven's will is hard to fathom, reason is difficult to deduce, and the span of mortal life cannot be known. But this year my grey hair is turning white, my loose teeth are falling out. I grow feebler every day, my mental powers are diminishing day by day, and before long I may follow you to the grave. If there is consciousness after death, I shall not be separated from you. If there is no consciousness, this sorrow will endure but for a little, and then no more sorrow for ever.

Your son is just ten, mine five. But if man can be cut off in his prime, how dare we hope that children in arms will grow up? Last year you wrote to me: "From time to time I suffer greatly from dropsy."

"That disease is common south of the Yangtse," I thought, and was not unduly alarmed. Did you die of this, or of some other illness?

Your letter was dated the seventeenth of the sixth month, but Meng told me that you died on the second of the month, while Geng Lan's report gives no date. I take it Meng's messenger did not ask your family, and Geng Lan did not think to mention it. So when Meng wrote he questioned the messenger, who gave him a wrong answer. Is this correct?

I have sent Jianzhong to make sacrifice to you and sent condolences to your children and foster-mother, asking her to stay there if she has the means till the period of mourning is over, when I shall go to fetch her. If she cannot do that, I shall bring her here now. I have told all the other servants to observe mourning. When I am able to rebury you, I shall lay your bones in our ancestral graveyard — only then can I rest content.

Alas! I did not know the hour of your illness, nor yet the day of your death. In life I could not watch over you at your side, and in death I could not weep over your corpse. At the funeral I could not touch your coffin, at the burial I could not stand by your grave. I have sinned against Heaven and caused your early death. I have failed in brotherly kindness, failed to help you in life or to be with you at the last — instead we were at opposite ends of the earth. In life your shadow could not cleave to my form, in death your spirit cannot enter my dreams. This is my fault, and mine alone. Heaven above, when will my sorrow cease? I shall take no further interest in human affairs, but find a few acres of land between the Yi and the Ying to pass the rest of my days. There I shall teach your son and mine, to make good men of them, and there I shall bring up our daughters till they reach the age of marriage. This will be all my care.

Ah, words fail me, but my love can never end. Do you hear me now, or has all consciousness left you? Alas! May your spirit come to the sacrifice!

A Farewell to Ou Ce

YANGSHAN is one of the poorest places on earth. Its precipitous crags are infested by tigers and leopards. Its fierce torrents are intersected by rocks sharper than swords and halberds, so that many boats veering from their course capsize or are wrecked. All is desert outside the county town, and the magistrate has no assistant. On the river bank, among the reeds and bamboos, live some dozen local officers' families with a bird-like tongue and barbarous appearance. At my arrival we had no common language, but had to draw on the ground to settle the amount of taxes or make appointments. There is no occasion for guests or travellers to call. Here I have stayed for the last six months, awaiting my punishment.

Now Ou Ce has pledged me his friendship. He came from Nan-hai by boat, and ascended the steps with an air of great dignity. As we sat and talked, he showed remarkable insight. Zhuang Zi said: "A man who has fled to the wilderness rejoices to hear human footsteps." How much more so when the visitor is Ou Ce! When he comes in and hears my comments on the classics or on morality, he is in raptures and seems to share my ideas. At times we rest in the shade of some noble tree, or sit on a rock by the stream to fish with rods. He takes pleasure in such pursuits, and appears able to renounce fame and profit and to rest content with poverty and obscurity.

In the New Year he will go home to see his parents. After emptying a pot of wine, I write this to mark his departure.

Verses for the Stone Tripod

ON the fourth day of the twelfth month of the seventh year of the Yuanhe era, * a priest of Hengshan named Xuanyuan Miming came down from the mountains. He was acquainted with Liu Shifu, a scholar from the same district, and as he heard that Liu was in the capital he went to spend a night at his house on his way to Taibai Mountain.

Hou Xi, a collator who had just won fame as a poet, was there to discuss poetry with Liu that night, and Miming sat down with them. This priest was remarkably ugly, with a white beard, dark face, long neck and scrawny throat, and he spoke with a southern accent. Hou Xi ignored him.

Suddenly that priest raised his eyebrows and spread out his clothes, pointing at the stone tripod on the stove.

"You claim to be a poet," he challenged Hou. "Can you write a verse on this with me?"

Liu had heard from some southerners that this priest, who was over ninety, could catch demons and goblins and hold captive sea-serpents, tigers and leopards. Although he could not be sure that this was true, he showed him respect on account of his great age. Not having known that the priest had literary tastes, he was delighted as he picked up a brush to write the opening couplet. He passed this to Hou, who took it eagerly and wrote two more lines.

"Is that the best you can do?" asked the priest with a laugh.

_____

* A.D. 812.

He put his hands in his sleeves and sat down with a shrug, his back against the north wall.

"I do not know the writing you use in the world," he told Liu. "Kindly take this down for me."

Then he chanted:

Obtuse as dragon-head fungus,
Bloated as porker's belly.

This verse, which he tossed off, was aimed at Hou. The two scholars exchanged surprised and embarrassed glances, and, meaning to outdo the priest in quantity, Liu wrote more and more couplets, passing them on to Hou. Hou racked his brains too, determined to beat the priest. He chanted each new couplet in a tragic voice, and hesitated with the brush in his hand, yet still he could produce nothing noteworthy. Each time he passed a couplet to the priest, sprawled on his seat Miming would call: "Take the pen, Liu! Here are my lines."

He tossed off some remarkable verses, quite out of the common, each a thrust at Liu or Hou, till Hou grew more and more exasperated. The two scholars made some dozen couplets apiece, but every time the priest capped them readily, and all his verses were barbed and had a sting.

After midnight Liu and Hou had to give up, having run out of ideas. They rose to apologize.

"You are no common man, master," they said. "We admit defeat and would like to be your pupils. We will never dare talk of poetry again."

But the priest exclaimed, "No, don't leave the poem unfinished. Take your pen, Liu. I'll finish it for you."

He chanted another forty words — eight lines — then told Liu to read them out.

"Is that finished now?" he demanded.

"Yes indeed," replied the two scholars.

"You are not worth talking to," retorted the priest. "That is not a poem. I wrote down to your level, not what I have learned from my master. You are not worthy to know what I can do — not only in literature either. As my words are wasted on you, I shall be silent."

The two scholars, overcome with awe, rose from their seats to bow.

"We dare not ask anything else, but one thing we long to know," they said. "You say, master, you cannot write like ordinary men. What script, pray, do you use? Please tell us this one thing."

The priest remained silent as if he had not heard them. Though they asked several times he made no reply, until they returned crestfallen to their seats. Then the priest fell asleep against the wall, and his snores resounded like thunder. The two scholars, pale with fear, dared scarcely breathe. Soon the morning drum sounded, and they fell asleep from exhaustion where they sat. When they woke, the sun was high in the sky and they looked round apprehensively for the priest, only to find him gone. They questioned the servant-boy.

"Just before dawn the priest went out, looking as if he would soon be back," said the boy. "I was surprised when he was away a long time; but when I went out to look for him he had disappeared."

The two scholars, filled with remorse, reproached themselves bitterly for losing him.

When they told me this story I did not know what manner of priest this was. I once heard of a hermit named Miming, and wonder if this can have been the same man.

Written on the Wall of the Assistant Magistrate's Office in Lantian

THE assistant magistrate's task is to help the magistrate and look into everything that goes on in his county. Under him are secretaries with various functions. But though his status is high, he is too cribbed and encumbered to take any action.

When a document has to be issued, the clerk brings it to him — made out. Holding the forepart of the scroll tightly rolled in his left hand, he pulls out its end with his right, swoops down on the assistant magistrate and looks at him askance.

"Your signature, please!" he says.

The assistant magistrate picks up his brush and signs with care in the allotted place, glancing at the clerk for reassurance.

"All in order," says the clerk, and withdraws.

The assistant magistrate dares not look into the matter and has no idea what is at issue. Though his position is high, he has less authority than the secretaries. But he is usually the first to be criticized, and is sometimes roundly abused for negligence. Is this why they created such a post?

Cui Sili of Boling cultivated the arts and stored his mind with learning, broadening and deepening his knowledge from day to day. At the beginning of the Zhenyuan era, when he went to prove his worth at a test in the capital, he came first in two examinations. At the beginning of the Yuan He era, for a word out of season he was dismissed from the Supreme Court where he was a judge, and transferred to be assistant magistrate of this county.

Upon his arrival he sighed and said: "This post is not too low, but I may not prove up to it."

When he found his hands tied he sighed again and said: "What an appointment! I am not thankless, but this is a thankless task."

Then he took pains not to be sharp or cutting, trod in his forerunners' steps, and stood on no ceremony. An old wall inscribed with names in the magistrate's office was so dilapidated, cracked and soiled that the writing on it was illegible. Cui replaced the beams and tiles, repaired and plastered the wall, and recorded all his predecessors' names. In the courtyard were four rows of old ash trees, and a thousand fine bamboos ranged solemnly by the south wall as if in attendance, while water gurgled past the steps. Cui cleaned the place thoroughly and planted two pines in front of his office, where he chanted poetry every day.

When asked any question he made haste to answer: "I am busy with affairs of state. Please go away!"

An Epitaph for Liu Zongyuan

LIU Zongyuan's cognomen was Zihou. One of his ancestors seven generations before him was Liu Qing, who served at court in the Toba Wei Dynasty and was made Lord of Jiyin. His great-grandfather's elder brother, Liu Shi, a prime minister in the Tang Dynasty, was executed with Zhu Suiliang and Han Yuan because they had offended Empress Wu during the reign of Emperor Gaozong. His father, Liu Zhen, gave up his post as doctor of ceremony in order to care for his mother at home, asking for a magistracy south of the Yangtse. Later he lost his position as censor because he would not fawn on a powerful noble, and was reinstated only after that noble's death. He was known for his probity, and all his friends were famous in their day.

Zihou was brilliant from boyhood, with a grasp of all branches of knowledge. Though still a lad at the time of his father's death, he had already distinguished himself by passing the examination in the capital. He was known as a worthy son of the house of Liu.

Later, having passed an examination, testing erudition and literary talent, he was made a secretary in Jixian Palace. Strikingly brilliant, fearless and incorruptible, he enforced his arguments with examples from the past and present, was well-versed in the classics, histories and hundred schools of thought, marshalled his facts as swiftly as the wind, and nearly always refuted his opponents. His fame spread far and wide, and he was greatly sought after. High officials competed to win him as their protégé, and had nothing but praise for him.

In the nineteenth year of the Zhenyuan era, * he was promoted from the assistant magistracy of Lantian to the post of supervising censor. Upon Emperor Shunzong's ascension to the throne, he was made a secretary of the Ministry of Ceremony. When later the ministers in power were punished, he was sent out as a prefect, but before reaching his post he was further demoted and made assistant prefect of Yongzhou. While there he worked harder than ever, studying and writing essays. He stored his mind with learning till his knowledge was limitless, and took his pleasure among the hills and streams.

During the Yuanhe era, he was recalled to the capital and sent out as a prefect again, this time to Liuzhou. Once there, he exclaimed: "How much work needs to be done here!"

He drew up regulations which accorded with local customs, and the people of the district abided by them. It was the custom there to give children as security for loans. If repayment was not made on time and the interest amounted to as much as the capital, the children were taken as servants. Liu thought of a way to redeem all these young people, directing that when the parents were too poor to pay the son should furnish the value of the loan in labour, after which he should be returned. The intendant of the circuit introduced this method to his other districts, and in one year nearly a thousand children were redeemed.

All the scholars south of Hengzhou and Xiangzhou looked upon Liu as their master, and those who had his personal advice on writing mastered the principles and produced good work.

When he was summoned to the capital and made a prefect, Liu

---

* A.D. 803.

Yuxi of Zhongshan was also appointed an official with a post at Bozhou.

Zihou shed tears and said: "Bozhou is not fit for human habitation. And his mother is still alive. I cannot bear to see him in such straits, unable to tell the old lady where he is going. It is out of the question for her to accompany her son."

He gladly risked heavy punishment by pleading for Liu Yuxi at court and asking to be sent to Bozhou himself instead of to Liuzhou. When this was reported to the emperor, Liu Yuxi was transferred to Lianzhou.

Ah! Adversity alone reveals a man's integrity! When all goes well, men may admire and befriend each other; eat, drink and take pleasure together; laugh at each other's jokes and flatter each other; clap hands or make a show of baring their hearts; point to the sun with tears in their eyes, and swear to be true till death — all this most convincingly. But when the least profit or risk is involved, be it slight as a hair, they will cold-shoulder you. If you fall into a pit, instead of stretching out a helping hand they will push you further in, or drop stones on you. This is happening every day. Even birds, beasts and barbarians would not stoop to such behaviour, yet these men pride themselves on their intelligence. They ought to blush when they hear of Zihou's deeds.

As a young man, Zihou championed the unfortunate and never spared himself, hoping to make a name for himself at once. That is why he was dismissed. After his demotion, as he had no influential friends to help him, he finally died in a desolate frontier region, his talents unused, his ideals unrealized. Had he held himself as much in check while a secretary as he did while a prefect, he would not have been dismissed. And after his dismissal, had some powerful official spoken for him, he could undoubtedly have been reinstated. But if he had not been banished for so long and reduced to such poverty, though he might have distinguished himself he would never have written the works he did — works which will be handed down to posterity. So even if his wish had come true and he had served as a general or minister, it is clear which of these achievements is worth more.

Zihou died on the eighth of the eleventh month of the fourteenth year of the Yuanhe era, * at the age of forty-seven. On the tenth of the seventh month of the fifteenth year, his body was interred beside his ancestors at Wannian.

He had two sons. The elder, Zhouliu, was just four. The younger, Zhouqi, was born after his father's death. He also had two daughters who were still children. His funeral expenses were met by the intendant of the circuit, Pei Xingli of Hedong. Pei is an upright and worthy gentleman. He befriended Zihou, who was a good friend to him too, and at the last it was he who saw to the funeral. Zihou's brother-in-law, Lu Zun, escorted the coffin to the graveyard at Wannian. Lu Zun comes from Zhuozhou. He is prudent and steady, devoted to his studies. After Zihou was demoted, Lu Zun went to live with him and remained with him till his death. After burying Zihou he continued to care for his family, showing himself a true friend from first to last.

The epitaph runs:

---

* A.D. 819.

> Here Liu Zongyuan doth dwell,
> Secure and sound
> Beneath the ground,
> May all his sons do well!

On Horses

ONLY after Bole* came into the world were there horses able to gallop one thousand *li*. Such horses are common, but a Bole is rare. So even fine steeds, if mishandled by slaves, will perish in their stables without being known as good horses.

A thousand-*li* horse may eat one bushel of grain at a meal, but if its groom does not know that this is what enables it to gallop a thousand *li* and fails to feed it enough, so that it lacks strength, it will not display its ability and natural gifts. Indeed, it may be no match for common horses; so how then can it gallop a thousand *li*?

If it is whipped and goaded on in the wrong way, too underfed to reveal its full worth, or if it neighs and the trainer treats it without understanding, then the rider may hold his whip over it exclaiming, "There are no good horses in the world!" But does this mean there are truly no good horses, or that he does not understand horses?

---

* A legendary figure in the seventh century B.C., Sun Yang or Bole was an authority on horses.

A Farewell to Monk Gao Xian

IF a man can lodge his intelligence within in such a way that the springs of action respond to the mind and are not deterred by circumstances, his spirit will remain whole and sound. Though outward things assail him, they will not clog his mind. This was the case with the government of Yao, Shun, Yu and Tang, with Yang Youji's archery, the slaughtering of the ox described by Zhuang Zi, Shi Kuang's music, Bian Que's medicine, Xiong Yiliao's catapult, Qiu's draughts, and Liu Ling's drinking. Their lifelong enjoyment of these things prevented them from thinking of externals. Those who take pleasure in outward things and keep changing their occupation have not entered the hall of knowledge or tasted its fare.

In the old days Zhang Xu was a master of the rustic style of writing, who learned no other art. Whenever his heart was moved, whether he was happy, angry or distressed, worried, pleased or at ease, enraged or wistful, drunk, bored or resentful, he would express it in his calligraphy. Whatever he saw, mountains and streams, cliffs and valleys, birds and beasts, insects and fish, flowers, fruit, trees or plants, the sun, the moon and the stars, the wind and the rain, flood and fire, thunder and lightning, song and dance, raging battles, all the changing phenomena of earth and heaven, whether inspiring or fearful, he would embody it in his writing. Thus his calligraphy was wellnigh divine, passing men's comprehension. By devoting his life to it he made his name.

But is Gao Xian today of the same mind as Zhang Xu when he

practises calligraphy? If you try to do what he did, lacking his spirit, you will never equal him. To write like Zhang Xu you must be clear on all issues, scrupulously exact, filled with a burning passion, sharply conflicting desires, and a strong sense of gain and loss. If you pour this out in your writing, you will be a second Zhang Xu.

Now Gao Xian is a Buddhist, unfettered by outward things, to whom life and death are one. His mind must be tranquil and dispassionate. He must have no worldly interests or earthly longings. But tranquillity combined with lack of interest result in complete surrender and abandon, untrammelled and unbridled. Then surely his calligraphy will express the principle of nothingness?

I have heard, though, that these Buddhists are skilled in creating illusions and in various arts. Gao Xian may have such skill, for all I know.

LIU YUXI

Liu Yuxi (772-842), a native of Luoyang in Henan, assumed a
variety of official posts after passing the highest imperial examinations in 791. He was later relegated to a lowly position in
Langzhou after being accused of having unsavoury political con-
nections. As a result of these activities in his early years, his
poetry frequently has a certain political dimension. He writes in
a simple and fresh manner and some of his poems possess the
flavour and cadence of folk songs.

Mosquitoes

ON sultry summer evenings when Orchid Hall stands open
At dusk mosquitoes raise a furious droning,
Their din first heard as fearful
As thunder rumbling from the southern mountains;
Clamouring, whirling, revelling in darkness,
The swarm obscures men's eyes, deceives their ears.
When flowers drip dew, the moon rides high,
How viciously they bite, driving sleep away;
A six-foot man am I, mere midges you,
But a horde against one you can wound me.
Natural seasons brooks no control,
I will hang a net over my bed to keep you out;
When with the dawn of autumn the air clears
You paltry pests will feed pheasants.

Recalling the Past at Mount Xisai

WANG Jun's galleons sailed down from Yizhou, *
Jinling's** kingly grandeur faded sadly away:
Chain-barricades sank fathoms deep in the Yangtse,

---

   * Wang Jun (206-285) led the troops of Jin down the Yangtse River from Sichuan
to conquer the Kingdom of Wu in 279.
  ** Jinling, present-day Nanjing in Jiangsu Province, was the capital of the Kingdom
of Wu (222-280) during the Three Kingdoms period.

Flags of surrender overspread the cliff.

Time and again men may lament the past;

The mountain remains unchanged, couched above cold river.

Now all within the Four Seas are one family,

By old ramparts autumn wind soughs through the reeds.

A Reply to Bai Juyi's[*] Poem at Our First Meeting at a Feast in Yangzhou

COLD and lonely the mountains of Ba, the rivers of Chu,[**]

Twenty-three years an exile,

Missing old friends, in vain I sang

The song of him who heard fluting,[***]

And home again am like the woodcutter[****]

Who found his axe-handle rotted.

By the sunken barge a thousand sails go past,

_____

[*] Bai Juyi (772-846), a famous Tang-dynasty poet, was a close friend of Liu Yuxi towards the end of his life.

[**] The mountains of Ba and the rivers of Chu refered to far-off regions in southwest China.

[***] The singer who heard fluting was Xiang Xiu of the third century, who was reminded by flute music of his dead friends and wrote a poem about them. Here Liu Yuxi was thinking of Wang Shuwen and others of his associates who had died.

[****] The woodcutter was Wang Zhi. According to a Jin-dynasty story, he went into the mountains to cut wood and stayed for a while with some immortals, returning home later only to find that his axe-handle had rotted away and none of his neighbours was left.

Before the withered tree all is green in spring;
Hearing your song today, sir,
I drink a cup of wine and take fresh heart.

Visiting Xuandu Temple

In the eleventh year of Yuanhe (816), on my recall to the capital from Langzhou, I wrote this poem for the amusement of the gentlemen who went out to enjoy the blossom.

RED dust sweeps men's faces on the royal highway,
None but declares he is back from seeing the blossom.
In Xuandu Temple are a thousand peach-trees
All planted since Master Liu left the capital.

Revisiting Xuandu Temple

When I served as secretary in the Department of State Farms in the twentieth year of Zhenyuan (805), this temple had no blossoming trees. That same year I was appointed prefect of Lianzhou, then demoted to be vice-prefect of Langzhou. Ten years later, when recalled to the capital, I heard it said on all sides that a Taoist priest had planted fairy peaches in this temple, making it seem enveloped in rosy clouds. I wrote the preceding poem to commemorate this before being sent to the provinces again.

Now, fourteen years later, having been summoned back to head

the Protocol Department, I have revisited Xuandu Temple. Not a
single peach-tree remains, only mallows and buckwheat wave in the
spring breeze. I have therefore written the following twenty-eight-
character poem while waiting to pay the temple further visits.

— In the third month of the second year of Dahe (828)

HALF the hundred-*mu* court is overgrown with moss;
Vanished the peach blossom, nothing blooms here but rape;
Gone, none knows where, the Taoist who planted the
    peaches,
But today Master Liu is back again.

A Willow Ballad

NORTH of the Pass, Qiang flutes played *Plum-Blossom*;
South of the Huai, Xiao Shan sang *Fragrant Cassia***
Play no more tunes, sir, of bygone dynasties
But hear the new *Willow Ballads*.

---

* The Qiangs were a nomadic people in China's northwest. *Plum-Blossom* was a
local folk melody.

** Xiao Shan, a protégé of the Prince of Huainan (179-122 B.C.), wrote a poem in
the traditional local style about fragrant cassia.

Bai Juyi

Bai Juyi (772-846), from Taiyuan in Shanxi, was one of the most influential poets of the mid-Tang. Like Han Yu, he placed great emphasis on the use of clear and intelligible language and he writes in a plain, accessible style. During his successful career as an administrator and adviser to the court, he presented many memorials proposing social reforms. He also emphasized the didactic function of literature and wrote numerous political satires as well as narrative poems exposing injustice. As with Han Yu and Du Fu, he was a vocal defender of Confucianism and critic of imperial ostentation and excess.

Song of Eternal Sorrow

APPRECIATING feminine charms,
The Han emperor sought a great beauty.
Throughout his empire he searched
For many years without success.
Then a daughter of the Yang family
Matured to womanhood.
Since she was secluded in her chamber,
None outside had seen her.
Yet with such beauty bestowed by fate,
How could she remain unknown?
One day she was chosen
To attend the emperor.
Glancing back and smiling,
She revealed a hundred charms.
All the powdered ladies of the six palaces
At once seemed dull and colourless.
One cold spring day she was ordered
To bathe in the Huaqing Palace baths.
The warm water slipped down
Her glistening jade-like body.
When her maids helped her rise,
She looked so frail and lovely,
At once she won the emperor's favour.
Her hair like a cloud,
Her face like a flower,
A gold hair-pin adorning her tresses.

Behind the warm lotus-flower curtain,
They took their pleasure in the spring night.
Regretting only the spring nights were too short;
Rising only when the sun was high;
He stopped attending court sessions
In the early morning.

Constantly she amused and feasted with him,
Accompanying him on his spring outings,
Spending all the nights with him.
Though many beauties were in the palace,
More than three thousand of them,
All his favours were centred on her.

Finishing her coiffure in the gilded chamber,
Charming, she accompanied him at night.
Feasting together in the marble pavilion,
Inebriated in the spring.

All her sisters and brothers
Became nobles with fiefs.
How wonderful to have so much splendour
Centred in one family!
All parents wished for daughters
Instead of sons!

The Li Mountain lofty pleasure palace
Reached to the blue sky.
The sounds of heavenly music were carried
By the wind far and wide.
Gentle melodies and graceful dances
Mingled with the strings and flutes;
The emperor never tired of these.

Then battle drums shook the earth,
The alarm sounding from Yuyang.
The Rainbow and Feather Garments Dance
Was stopped by sounds of war.
Dust filled the high-towered capital,
As thousands of carriages and horsemen
Fled to the southwest.
The emperor's green-canopied carriage
Was forced to halt,
Having left the west city gate
More than a hundred *li*.
There was nothing the emperor could do,
At the army's refusal to proceed.
So she with the moth-like eyebrows
Was killed before his horses.
Her floral-patterned gilded box
Fell to the ground, abandoned and unwanted,
Like her jade hair-pin
With the gold sparrow and green feathers.
Covering his face with his hands,
He could not save her.
Turning back to look at her,
His tears mingled with her blood.
Yellow dust filled the sky;
The wind was cold and shrill.
Ascending high winding mountain paths,
They reached the Sword Pass,
At the foot of the Emei Mountains.
Few came that way.

Their banners seemed less resplendent;
Even the sun seemed dim.
Though the rivers were deep blue,
And the Sichuan mountains green,
Night and day the emperor mourned.
In his refuge when he saw the moon,
Even it seemed sad and wan.
On rainy nights, the sound of bells
Seemed broken-hearted.
Fortunes changed, the emperor was restored.
His dragon-carriage started back.
Reaching the place where she died,
He lingered, reluctant to leave.
In the earth and dust of Mawei Slope,
No lady with the jade-like face was found.
The spot was desolate.
Emperor and servants exchanged looks,
Their clothes stained with tears.
Turning eastwards towards the capital,
They led their horses slowly back.
The palace was unchanged on his return,
With lotus blooming in the Taiye Pool
And willows in the Weiyang Palace.
The lotus flowers were like her face;
The willows like her eyebrows.
How could he refrain from tears
At their sight?
The spring wind returned at night;
The peach and plum trees blossomed again.

Plane leaves fell in the autumn rains.

Weeds choked the emperor's west palace;

Piles of red leaves on the unswept steps.

The hair of the young musicians of the Pear Garden

Turned to grey.

The green-clad maids of the spiced chambers

Were growing old.

At night when glow-worms flitted in the pavilion

He thought of her in silence.

The lonely lamp was nearly extinguished,

Yet still he could not sleep.

The slow sound of bells and drums

Was heard in the long night.

The Milky Way glimmered bright.

It was almost dawn.

Cold and frosty the paired love-bird tiles;

Chilly the kingfisher-feathered quilt

With none to share it.

Though she had died years before,

Even her spirit was absent from his dreams.

A priest from Linqiong came to Chang'an,

Said to summon spirits at his will.

Moved by the emperor's longing for her,

He sent a magician to make a careful search.

Swift as lightning, through the air he sped,

Up to the heavens, below the earth, everywhere.

Though they searched the sky and nether regions,

Of her there was no sign.

Till he heard of a fairy mountain

In the ocean of a never-never land.
Ornate pavilions rose through coloured clouds,
Wherein dwelt lovely fairy folk.
One was named Taizhen,
With snowy skin and flowery beauty,
Suggesting that this might be she.
When he knocked at the jade door
Of the gilded palace's west chamber,
A fairy maid, Xiaoyu, answered,
Reporting to another, Shuangcheng.
On hearing of the messenger
From the Han emperor,
She was startled from her sleep
Behind the gorgeous curtain.
Dressing, she drew it back,
Rising hesitantly.
The pearl curtains and silver screens
Opened in succession.
Her cloudy tresses were awry,
Just summoned from her sleep.
Without arranging her flower headdress,
She entered the hall.
The wind blew her fairy skirt,
Lifting it, as if she still danced
The Rainbow and Feather Garments Dance.
But her pale face was sad,
Tears filled her eyes,
Like a blossoming pear tree in spring,
With rain drops on its petals.

Controlling her feelings and looking away,
She thanked the emperor.
Since their parting she had not heard
His voice nor seen his face.
While she had been his first lady,
Their love had been ruptured.
Many years had passed
On Penglai fairy isle.
Turning her head,
She gazed down on the mortal world.
Chang'an could not be seen,
Only mist and dust.
She presented old mementos
To express her deep feeling.
Asking the messenger to take
The jewel box and the golden pin.
"I'll keep one half of the pin and box;
Breaking the golden pin
And keeping the jewel lid.
As long as our love lasts
Like jewels and gold,
We may meet again
In heaven or on earth."
Before they parted
She again sent this message,
Containing a pledge
Only she and the emperor knew.
In the Palace of Eternal Youth
On the seventh of the seventh moon,

Alone they had whispered
To each other at midnight:
"In heaven we shall be birds
Flying side by side.
On earth flowering sprigs
On the same branch!"
Heaven and earth may not last for ever,
But this sorrow was eternal.

Lodging in a Village North of the Hill of the Purple Pavilion

IN the morning I climbed the Peak of the Purple Pavilion,
In the evening I lodged in the village under the hill;
The village elder was pleased that I had come
And in my honour opened a jar of wine;
Yet before the cups reached our lips,
Rough soldiers burst through the gate;
In purple uniform, with sword and axe,
Ten or more, an unruly band.
They snatched the wine from our table,
They seized the food from our plates;
My host made way and stood behind them,
His hands in his sleeves as though himself a guest.
In the yard was a noble tree
Planted thirty springs before;

In vain my host tried to save it,
They took their axes and felled it at the root.
They claimed they were collecting timber for building
And belonged to the Armies of the Holy Plan. *
Better not complain, my host,
For their commander now stands high in favour.

My New Wadded Gown

WHITE as snow the Guangxi cloth,
Soft as clouds the Suzhou silk;
The thick material wadded with silk floss
Makes me a good warm gown.
Wrapped in its folds I sit from dawn till dusk,
Covered with it at night I sleep till day,
Forgetting the months of harsh winter,
My whole body as warm as in spring.
But one night a sudden thought strikes me,
I get up, fingering my gown, to pace the room.
Now men should prize happiness for all
Above the well-being of one.
Oh, for a gown which spreads ten thousand *li*
To cover and enfold the four corners of the earth,
Making all as warm and comfortable as I,
None left cold beneath the vault of heaven!

---

* Two forces of imperial guards commanded by a eunuch.

The Lady of Shangyang Palace

THE lady of Shangyang, lady of Shangyang!
Her bloom gone, age creeps on, white grows her hair.
The palace gate is guarded by eunuchs in green —
How many springs have passed since she was immured there?
First chosen at the end of Minghuang's reign,
Sixteen when she came to the palace, now she is sixty;
The hundred beauties and more brought in with her
Have flickered out through the long years, leaving her
    alone.
She remembers how she swallowed her grief and left home;
They helped her into the carriage, forbade her to cry;
Once in the palace, they said, she would be favoured,
For her face was fair as a lotus, her bosom like jade.
But before her royal master could see her face,
The Lady Yang cast jealous eyes on her,
And consigned her secretly to Shangyang Palace
To pass the rest of her days in a lonely chamber.
In that empty room the autumn nights were long,
Long, sleepless nights when it seemed dawn would never
    come;
Dim, dim the lamp threw her shadow on the wall,
Chill, chill the rain pattered all night on her window;
The spring days dragged so slowly,
As alone she sat all day long, and dusk would not fall.
How she wearied of the palace orioles' warbling,
Long past envying the swallows in pairs on the beams;

Then orioles and swallows were gone and all was still;
Spring passed and autumn came, she lost count of time;
Only, watching the bright moon above the palace,
Four hundred times and more she has seen it wax and wane,
And today she is the oldest palace lady —
The sovereign, far off, gives her the title *Shangshu*. *
Her shoes are pointed, her gown tightly fitted,
With a dark pencil she draws her long slender eyebrows,
And people outside would laugh if they could see her,
For this is the fashion of the last years of Tianbao.
What grief she has known, the lady of Shangyang,
Grief in girlhood, grief in old age!
What can come of this lifetime of grief?
Know, then, that Lü Xiang wrote *An Ode to the Fair Maid***
And today we sing of this white-haired lady of Shangyang.

The Old Man with the Broken Arm

IN Xinfeng there lives an old man of eighty-eight,
His hair, his eyebrows and beard as white as snow;
As his grandson's grandson helps him past the inn
His left arm is on the boy's shoulder, his right hangs useless.
In what year did this happen? I ask the old man.

---

* i.e. secretary-general.
** At the end of the Tianbao period there were Flower-and-bird Messengers who se-
cretly picked beautiful girls for the emperor. Lü Xiang presented his ode to the
emperor as a veiled protest against this practice.

What caused him to be maimed?

He told me Xinfeng was the home of his ancestors,

And here he lived in a good reign free of wars;

He often heard the singing and luting of court musicians,

With no knowledge of standards and lances, bows and arrows.

Later on great armies were raised in the Tianbao period,

One out of every three men must go to the wars,

And where would the conscripts be sent?

In the fifth month they must set off ten thousand *li* to Yunnan;

There in Yunnan, rumour said, by the River Lu,

Malarial mists rose when pepper flowers fell,

And the army must wade through water scalding hot;

Of every ten two or three would die in the crossing.

So north and south of the village rose bitter lamenting

As sons took leave of their parents, men left their wives;

For from all those campaigns against the southern tribesmen,

Of the thousands who went not one was known to return.

He was twenty-four at the time,

And his name was on the war ministry's list;

So late one night, unknown to all,

With a great stone he shattered his arm;

Then unable to bend a bow or bear a standard,

He was sent to Yunnan but discharged.

Of course, breaking the bone and tearing the tendon were painful,

But that was the way to get discharged and go home.

It is sixty years now since this arm was disablcd,
He has lost the use of one limb but his life has been spared.
Even now on damp, chilly nights of wind and rain,
Pain keeps him awake till dawn;
But in spite of the pain he has no regret
Rejoicing to have lived on till old age.
Failing this, he would have died by the River Lu,
His spirit lonely in death, his bones unburied,
A ghost in far-off Yunnan longing for home,
Wailing by the common grave of ten thousand dead.
Ponder well, my lord, the words of this old man.
Know that Song Jing, chief minister in the Kaiyuan period,
To deter warfare rewarded no feats at the frontier,
While Yang Guozhong after him in the Tianbao period
Sought the imperial favour through frontier fighting —
Yet all he achieved was popular discontent.
Ask the old man with the broken arm at Xinfeng
What he has to say about this.

The Old Man of Duling

EACH year the old man of Duling
Tills a hundred *mu* or more of poor barren land.
There is no rain in the third month, only dry winds,
Before the wheat puts forth ears it withers and dies;
There is frost in the ninth month, the autumn cold comes
    early,

Before the green millet can ripen it is blasted.
The local officer knows this but will not report it,
Harshly he makes his levies to win himself credit.
Mulberry trees are mortgaged, land sold to pay taxes,
But where are next year's food and clothing to come from?
They have stripped the coat from my back,
They have snatched the grain from my mouth;
These are wolves destroying life and property,
It is not only fanged beasts that devour men's flesh.
Someone has sent a memorial to the throne,
The emperor sees the injustice and has compassion;
On white hempen paper comes down his virtuous decree:
All the land near Chang'an is exempted this year from taxes.
But not until yesterday did the headman come to our doors
With this decree in his hand to tell the whole village;
By then nine households out of ten had paid,
So our sovereign's kindness was wasted!

The Brocade of the South

WHAT can compare with the brocade of the south?
No gauze or satin this,
But rather the waterfall on Mount Tiantai
That plunges forty-five feet in the bright moonlight;
It has the rarest patterns,
White smoke misting the ground and snowy clusters of flow-
    ers.

Who weaves such brocade? Who wears it?

Poor girls by the streams of Yue, ladies in the palace.

Last year the imperial eunuch passed on the emperor's order:

Designs from Heaven should be woven on earth.

Here are flights of wild geese beyond the clouds in autumn,

Dyed the colour of water south of the Yangtse in spring.

The sleeves are wide, the skirt long;

Cut with golden scissors and smoothly pressed,

Its rare brightness is a foil for the strange designs,

And at every turn the flowers on it flash and quiver.

The dancer of Zhaoyang Palace is high in the emperor's favour,

A set of her spring garments costs a thousand pieces of gold;

Once powder and sweat have stained them she discards them,

To be trailed through the dust and mud for all she cares.

To weave this brocade of the south is no easy task;

This is no ordinary satin or silk;

Holding many of these fine threads makes a girl's hand ache,

And the shuttle must clack a thousand times to weave less than one foot.

If the lady singing and dancing in Zhaoyang Palace

Could see the weaving, she would surely care for the brocade!

The Old Charcoal Seller

THE old man who sells charcoal
Cuts wood and fires his wares on the South Hill,
His face streaked with dust and ashes, grimed with smoke,
His temples grizzled, his ten fingers blackened.
The little money he makes is hardly enough
For clothing for his back, food for his belly;
But though his coat is thin he hopes for winter —
Cold weather will keep up the price of fuel.
At night a foot of snow falls outside the city,
At dawn his charcoal cart crushes ruts in the ice;
By the time the sun is high,
The ox is tired out and the old man hungry,
They rest in the slush outside the south gate of the market.
Then up canter two riders; who can they be?
Palace heralds in yellow jackets and white shirts;
They wave a decree, shout that these are imperial orders;
They turn the cart, hoot at the ox and drag it north.
A whole cartload of charcoal, more than a thousand catties,
Yet they drive it off to the palace and he must accept
The strip of red gauze and the ten feet of silk
Which they fasten to the ox's horns as payment!

The Salt Merchant's Wife

THE salt merchant's wife has plenty of money;
She needn't farm, breed silk-worms or weave.
Wherever she goes she always has a home;
The boat her house, wind and water her home.
From a poor Yangzhou family,
She married a big merchant west of the Yangtse.
Growing rich, many gold hair-pins adorn her glossy hair;
Growing plump, the silver bracelet on her arm is tight.
She orders about her servants and maids;
Yet how did she become so wealthy?
Her husband has been a salt merchant for fifteen years;
Not controlled by the district, but only by the emperor.
Each year when the salt monopoly profit goes to the state,
The smaller share is for the government,
The larger one for private hands.
So the government profits less than private people,
But the ministry far away is not aware of this.
Besides, fish and rice arc cheap in the Yangtse Valley;
With red herring, yellow oranges and fragrant rice.
She can eat well, dress herself up and lean by the stern-
   tower,
Her red cheeks glowing like a blooming flower.
How lucky she is to have married a salt merchant!
Good food every day, fine clothes all year round.
But who's the source of these fine clothes and food?

She ought to thank Sang Hongyang for them.*
Sang Hongyang died a long time ago.
But he wasn't only in the Han Dynasty,
There are such people around today too!

Proud Eunuchs

THEIR proud airs seemed to fill the road,
Dust reflected their gleaming saddled horses.
When I inquired who they were,
People answered they were palace eunuchs.
Red insignia signified the rank of minister,
And purple insignia a general.
Boasting of their feast at the army headquarters,
They galloped away like fleeting clouds.
Their goblets overflowed with choicest wines;
Their dishes were delicacies from land and sea.
For fruit, they peeled oranges from Dongting Hill;
For fish, they ate slices from those of Lake Tianchi.
Satiated with food, they felt at their ease.
Inebriated by wine, their spirits soared.
Yet this year saw a drought south of the river;
And in Quzhou, men were eating men.

---

* Sang Hongyang in the Han Dynasty started the salt and iron government
monopoly.

Song and Dance

THE year draws to its close in the land of Qin, *
A great snow fills the imperial capital;
And in the snow, leaving court,
Are noble lords in purple and vermilion.
The noble can enjoy the wind and snow,
The wealthy have no fear of cold and hunger;
All their care is to build great mansions,
All their task the pursuit of pleasure.
Horses and carriages throng the vermilion entrance,
Song and dance last on by red candle-light in the pavilion
In high delight the guests sit close together,
Heated with wine they throw off their thick furs.
The host is head of the Board of Punishments,
The guest of honour is the Lord High Justice.
At midday the music and drinking start
And midnight sees no end to the merriment.
What do they care that in Wenxiang Gaol
Prisoners are freezing to death?

---

* Present-day Shaanxi, where Chang'an, the Tang capital, was situated.

Buying Flowers

ALMOST late spring in the imperial city;
Noise and bustle from passing carriages and horses.
People said that peonies were in blossom,
Following each other to buy the flowers.
Expensive or cheap, no fixed price, except according to
  quantity;
Five hundred bright red blossoms cost five lengths of silk.
Overhead were awnings and curtains for shelters;
Around them were bamboo fences for protection.
Sprayed with water and their roots sealed with mud;
When they were removed, they still retained their beauty.
Every family accepted this, none questioning it was wrong.
Then an old villager came to the market.
Head bowed, he sighed to himself, though none knew why.
He sighed because the cost of a bunch of deep red flowers
Was the same as the taxes paid by ten peasant families.

My Village in the Bitter Weather

IN the twelfth month in the eighth year of Yuanhe*
Snow fell thickly for five days in succession.
All the bamboos and cypresses perished in the cold,

---

* The eighth year of Yuanhe was in A.D. 813, when the poet retired from office
and stayed in his village home to observe the mourning period after his mother's
death.

What then happened to those ill-clad peasants?
When I saw those village families,
Out of ten, eight or nine were poor.
The north wind was piercing as a sword,
Yet they had insufficient clothing for their bodies.
They could only light a fire with brambles and weeds,
Sitting sadly at night to await the dawn.
Thus I saw during a severe spell of cold,
The peasants endured an agonizing time.
In those days I had a thatched hut with closed doors,
A fur coat with a cloth cover and raw silk bedding;
I had extra warmth, whether I sat or slept.
So I was fortunate to escape hunger and cold;
Nor did I have to toil in the fields.
Considering this, I feel ashamed,
And ask myself, what sort of person I am.

Song of the Lute Player

In 815, the tenth year of the Yuanhe period, I was demoted to the assistant prefectship of Jiujiang. The next autumn while seeing a friend off at Penpu, I heard someone strumming a lute in a boat at night, playing with the touch of a musician from the capital. I found upon inquiry that the lutist was a courtesan from Chang'an who had learned from the musicians Mu and Cao but growing old and losing her looks, she had married a merchant. Then I ordered drinks and asked her to play a few tunes. After playing, in deep distress, she told me of the pleasures of her youth and said now that her beauty had faded she was drifting from place to place by rivers and lakes.

*In my two years as an official away from the capital I had been re-
signed enough, my mind at peace but moved by her tale that night I
began to take my demotion and exile to heart. So I wrote a long poem and presented it to her. It has six hundred and twelve words and
I call it the "Song of the Lute Player".*

BY the Xunyang River a guest is seen off one night;

Chill the autumn, red the maple leaves and the reeds are in
    flower;

The host alights from his horse, the guest is aboard,

They raise their cups to drink but have no music.

Drunk without joy, in sadness they must part;

At the time of parting the river seems steeped in moonlight;

Suddenly out on the water a lute is heard;

The host forgets to turn back, the guest delays going.

Seeking the sound in the dark, we ask who is the player.

The lute is silent; hesitant the reply.

Rowing closer, we ask if we may meet the musician,

Call for more wine, trim the lamp and resume our feast;

Only after a thousand entreaties does she appear,

Her face half hidden behind the lute in her arms.

She tunes up and plucks the strings a couple of times,

Touching our hearts before ever the tune is played;

Each chord strikes a pensive note

As if voicing the disillusion of a lifetime;

Her head is bent, her fingers stray over the strings

Pouring out the infinite sorrows of her heart.

Lightly she pinches in the strings, slowly she strums and
   plucks them;
First *The Rainbow Garments*, then *The Six Minor Notes*.
The high notes wail like pelting rain,
The low notes whisper like soft confidences;
Wailing and whispering interweave
Like pearls large and small cascading on plate of jade,
Like a warbling oriole gliding below the blossom,
Like a mountain brook purling down a bank,
Till the brook turns to ice, the strings seem about to snap,
About to snap, and for one instant all is still
Only an undertone of quiet grief
Is more poignant in the silence than any sound;
Then a silver bottle is smashed, out gushes the water,
Mailed riders charge, their swords and lances clang!
When the tune ends, she draws her plectrum full across
And the four strings give a sound like the tearing of silk.
Right and left of the boat all is silence —
We see only the autumn moon, silver in mid-stream.
Pensively she puts the plectrum between the strings,
Straightens her clothes, rises and composes herself.
She is, she says, a girl from the capital
Whose family once lived at the foot of Toad Hill.
At thirteen she learned to play the lute
And ranked first among the musicians;
Her playing was admired by the old masters,
Her looks were the envy of other courtesans;
Youths from wealthy districts vied in their gifts to engage
   her,

A single song brought her countless rolls of red silk;

Jewelled and silver trinkets were smashed as men used them

to mark the beat;

Silk skirts as red as blood were stained by spilt wine.

Pleasure and laughter from one year to the next,

While the autumn moon and spring breeze passed unheeded.

Then her brother joined the army, her aunt died,

The days and nights slipped by and her beauty faded,

No more carriages and horsemen thronged her gate,

And growing old she became a merchant's wife.

All the merchant's thought is of profit: to seek it he leaves

her.

Two months ago he went to Fuliang to buy tea,

Leaving her alone in the boat at the mouth of the river;

All around the moonlight is bright, the river is cold,

And late at night, dreaming of her girlhood,

She cries in her sleep, staining her rouged cheeks with tears.

The music of her lute has made me sigh,

And now she tells this plaintive tale of sorrow;

We are both ill-starred, drifting on the face of the earth;

No matter if we were strangers before this encounter.

Last year I bade the imperial city farewell;

A demoted official, I lay ill in Xunyang;

Xunyang is a paltry place without any music,

For one year I heard no wind instruments, no strings.

Now I live on the low, damp flat by the River Pen,

Round my house yellow reeds and bitter bamboos grow rife;

From dawn till dusk I hear no other sounds

But the wailing of night-jars and the moaning of apes.

On a day of spring blossom by the river or moonlit night in
   autumn

I often call for wine and drink alone;

Of course, there are rustic songs and village pipes,

But their shrill discordant notes grate on my ears;

Tonight listening to your luting

Was like hearing fairy music; it gladdened my ears.

Don't refuse, but sit down and play another tune,

And I'll write a *Song of the Lute Player* for you.

Touched by my words, she stands there for some time,

Then goes back to her seat and plays with quickened tempo

Music sadder far than the first melody,

And at the sound not a man of us has dry eyes.

The assistant prefect of Jingzhou is so moved

That his blue coat is wet with tears.

Walking by Qiantang Lake* in Spring

NORTH of Gushan Monastery, west of the Jia Pavilion.

Water brims level with the bank, the clouds hang low;

Here and there, the first orioles are disputing for sunny
   trees,

---

* The West Lake in Hangzhou.

While young swallows, just down from the eaves, peck in
   the spring mud.
The riot of flowers begins to dazzle the eye,
The short grass barely covers the horses' hooves;
I love best the east of the lake, and could stroll for ever
On that white-sand embankment shaded by green willows.

LIU ZONGYUAN

Liu Zongyuan (773-819), from Yuncheng County in Shanxi, is also considered one of the great prose stylists of the Tang. His scholarship and literary talent earned him a reputation early in his career and he held many official posts. His membership of a political group which attempted to persuade the emperor to introduce certain reforms led to exile in Yongzhou, Hunan, more than three thousand *li* from the capital. He was subsequently banished to the even more remote province of Guizhou where he died. He produced his finest writing after his demotion at the age of thirty-two. Liu Zongyuan was an advocate of the movement led by Han Yu to reform the mannered and affected prose style then prevalent.

Some Incidents from the Life of Marshal Duan

(A Report for the Official Historians)

WHILE Marshal Duan was prefect of Jingzhou, the Prince of Fenyang* was the deputy commander-in-chief of the empire, residing in Pu County. His son Guo Xi, the imperial secretary and commander of the forces stationed at Binzhou, let his troops run wild. The profligates and ruffians of that district paid bribes to be enrolled in his army so that they could do as they pleased, and the local officials dared not interfere. Bands raided the market each day and, unless they got all they wanted, would beat the vendors, break their arms and legs, or throw pots and pans, pitchers and dishes all over the street before strolling off arm in arm. They even knocked down and killed a pregnant woman. Bai Xiaode, governor of Binzhou area, was seriously concerned, but because of the prince he dared not say anything.

Duan went from Jingzhou to make a report to the governor, hoping that steps would be taken to deal with the situation.

"The Son of Heaven has entrusted some of his subjects to you, sir," he said. "Yet you stand by and watch them suffer. What if there is a riot?"

"What would you advise?" asked the governor.

"I am very well off at Jingzhou, with little to do," replied Duan. "But I cannot stand seeing men murdered in time of peace,

---

* Guo Ziyi, who crushed An Lushan's rebellion in the middle of the eighth century.

and strife stirred up at the border. If you will appoint me provost-marshal, I can end this trouble for you and avert this danger from the citizens here."

"Very good," said Governor Bai. "So let it be."

A month after Duan took up his new post, seventeen of Guo Xi's soldiers, demanding drink, went to the market and stabbed an old wine vendor, smashing his vats so that the wine flowed into the gutters. Duan sent troops to arrest these seventeen men, and had their heads cut off and impaled on spears which were planted outside the market-place. At that, Guo Xi's soldiers set up a great clamour and put on their armour. Then the governor took fright and summoned Duan.

"What shall we do?" he asked.

"Have no fear," said Duan. "Let me speak to the troops."

The governor gave him an escort of several dozen men, but he sent them all away. Leaving his sword behind, and with a lame old man as his groom, he went to Guo Xi's camp. When armed men came out, he laughed.

"Why put on armour to kill an old trooper?" he asked as he entered the gate. "I have brought my head with me."

The armed men were taken aback.

"What harm has the imperial secretary done you?" asked Duan. "Why do you want to ruin the Guo family? Report my arrival to Secretary Guo and tell him I wish to speak to him."

Then Guo Xi came out to see him.

"The Prince of Fenyang is famed throughout the world," the marshal told him. "You should see to it that his reputation endures. Yet now you are letting your troops run wild and make trouble, creating a disturbance at the border; but if anyone is blamed, it will be the Prince of Fenyang. The young scoundrels of this district have bribed their way into your army, and are killing and injuring people. Unless a stop is put to this, in a few days there will be a riot, and you will be responsible. And everyone will say that because you rely on your father's might you do not control your troops. Then what will be left of your family's reputation?"

Before he had finished, Guo Xi bowed in contrition.

"I am grateful to you for telling me the truth," he said. "I am very much in your debt. I will order my troops as you think best."

Then he turned and spoke sternly to his men:

"Take off your armour and lay down your weapons! Go back to your squads and companies! Whoever creates disturbances will be killed!"

"I have not yet dined," said the marshal. "May I trouble you for a simple meal?" And after eating he said, "I am not feeling well. I would like to spend the night here."

Bidding his groom come back the following day, he lay down to sleep in the camp. Guo Xi did not remove his clothes that night, but warned his scouts to keep a good watch and protect the marshal. The next morning Guo Xi accompanied Duan to the governor's office to tender apologies and ask for a chance to make good. And after that there was no more trouble in Binzhou.

Before this, when Duan was serving as land officer at Jingzhou, a general there named Jiao Lingchen seized several thousand *mu* of private land, and ordered his tenants:

"When you harvest your grain, you must give me half of it."

That year there was a serious drought, and even the grass there withered. One of his tenants reported this to Jiao.

"All I care about is my share," retorted the general. "Don't talk to me about drought."

And he pressed still harder for payment. But even if this peasant had starved he could not have paid; so he informed Duan, who wrote a gently worded judgement and sent men to Jiao to persuade him to waive his claim. In great anger, Jiao summoned his tenant.

"Do you think I am afraid of Duan?" he shouted. "How dare you report me to him?"

He snatched up the judgement and spread it on the peasant's back, then gave him twenty strokes with a great cudgel. The man was carried, half dead, to Duan's office.

"It was I who brought this on you!" exclaimed Duan, shedding tears.

He fetched water to wash the blood off the peasant's back, tore up his own linen to bind his wounds, administered medicine himself, and fed him both morning and evening before eating himself. Then, unknown to the poor man, he sold his own horse to buy grain to pay his rent.

A courageous and upright man named Yin Shaorong was then commander of the Huaixi garrison. He went to see Jiao, and abused him roundly.

"Are you a man?" he demanded. "All Jingzhou is bare and parched, and men are starving to death, yet you insist on getting your grain and beat an innocent man with a great cudgel. Duan is a kind-hearted, honest, noble man, yet you have no respect for him. He sold his only horse at a loss in order to buy grain to pay you, and you took it quite brazenly. You have disregarded a heaven-sent calamity, opposed a respectable gentleman, beaten an innocent man, and taken a good man's grain, leaving him with no horse to ride. How can you face heaven and earth? How can you hold up your head before your slaves?"

Though Jiao was a violent man, when he heard this he was humbled. The sweat poured down his face, and he could not eat.

"I cannot look Duan in the face again," he said.

He died one night of remorse.

Later, when Duan was promoted from Jingzhou to the post of minister of agriculture, he warned his relatives not to accept any gifts from Marshal Zhu Ci when they passed Qizhou. As soon as they reached that district, Zhu Ci did indeed send them three hundred rolls of brocade; but though Duan's son-in-law Wei Wu declined again and again, he was forced to accept the gift.

"So you did not take my advice!" cried the marshal angrily when they reached the capital.

"My rank was too low to refuse," said Wei Wu, and apologized.

"Still, this must not remain in my house," declared the marshal.

So he stowed the gift over a beam in his office in the ministry of agriculture. By the time Zhu Ci styled himself emperor, the marshal had died. But his officers told Zhu Ci of this incident, and when he bade them bring back his gift he found the original seal unbroken.

The marshal is usually praised as an impetuous soldier who won fame throughout the empire because he did not fear death. His integrity is not known. In my former travels up and down Qizhou and Binzhou, past Zhending and north to Maling, to visit all the outposts and garrisons, I liked to ask old soldiers for stories, and they all had tales of Duan. The marshal, they said, appeared very easy-going, and walked with bent head and folded arms. His speech was mild, his behaviour unassuming, and he never lost his temper; indeed, people often took him for a scholar. But if he found that injustice had been done, he would not rest till he had set it right.

During the visit here of Prefect Cui of Yongzhou — a man of the utmost probity — I checked these tales about the marshal with him, and found them all to be true. Fearing lest these incidents be forgotten and lost if not compiled by the official historians, I am making this report to those in charge.

The Snake-Catcher

The country around Yongzhou yields a curious snake — black with white spots. Any plant it touches dies, and its bite is fatal. But if caught and dried for medicine, it cures leprosy, palsy and boils, heals putrid sores and checks all noxious humours. In earlier times it was decreed that two snakes should be presented each year to the imperial physician, and that those who captured them should be exempted from other taxes. So the people of Yongzhou made every effort to catch them.

I questioned a man named Jiang, whose family had made a living in this way for three generations.

"My grandfather died of snake-bite, so did my father," he told me in great distress. "Now I have followed in their steps for twelve years, and narrowly escaped death several times."

I pitied him.

"If you hate this calling," I said, "I can ask the authorities to release you from it and let you pay land tax instead. What do you say?"

Jiang was appalled. Tears welled up in his eyes.

"Have pity on me, sir!" he cried. "Though this is a wretched life, it is better than paying taxes. If not for these snakes, I would have come to grief long ago. For the sixty years that my grandfather, father and I have lived here, our neighbours have been more and more hard put to it every day. When their soil is exhausted, their savings spent, they leave their homes lamenting to fall hungry and thirsty by the wayside; or toil winter and summer in the wind and rain, contracting diseases till their corpses pile up. Of my grandfather's generation, not one in ten is left; not three in ten of my father's; and not five in ten of those who were my neighbours twelve years ago. The rest are dead or gone while I alone live on — because I catch snakes. When those bullying tax-collectors come to our district, they bellow and curse from east to west and rampage from north to south, making such a fearful din that the very birds and dogs have no peace. Then I tiptoe from my bed to look into my pitcher, but breathe freely again at the sight of my snakes and lie down once more. I feed my snakes carefully, and present them in due season, then come home to enjoy the fruits of my fields in comfort. I risk death twice a year, but live happily for the rest, unlike my neighbours who face death every day. Though I die tomorrow, I shall have outlived most of them. How could I hate this calling?"

At this I pitied the fellow even more.

I used to doubt that saying of Confucius: Tyranny is more rapacious than a tiger. But Jiang's case convinced me of its truth. Alas, to think that taxation can prove more dire than a poisonous snake! So I have written this essay for those who study conditions in the countryside.

The Bear

THE deer is afraid of the jackal, the jackal of the tiger, and the tiger of the bear. The bear has shaggy hair and can stand on two legs. Its great strength makes it most dangerous to men.

South of the land of Chu lived a hunter who could imitate the cries of all beasts on his bamboo pipe. One day, taking his bow and arrows and carrying embers in a pitcher, he climbed the hills to make the sound of a deer, so that when a deer came, attracted by the cry, he could show his light and shoot it. A jackal ran up, however, on hearing this cry; so the hunter took fright and made the noise of a tiger. As soon as the jackal left, though, a tiger arrived; then the hunter, more frightened than ever, made the noise of a bear. At that the tiger fled, but a bear came in search of a mate. Finding a man, it seized him with both paws, tore him limb from limb, and ate him.

All those who rely on some power not their own will meet their doom.

Song Qing

SONG Qing had a shop in the medicine market in the west end of Chang'an. He stocked good drugs, for he dealt fairly with the vendors and they took him whatever they found in the mountains or marshes. And when the Chang'an physicians used his drugs in their prescriptions they always proved efficacious; so all spoke well of him. Then the sick applied to him for physic too, hoping for a speedy cure, and Song Qing supplied them gladly. Though a customer brought no money, he would still give him the best. Notes of hand piled up, yet he never pressed for payment; and even strangers could get credit from him. At the end of the year, if he thought someone could not pay him, he would burn his notes and say no more about them. This amazed all the tradesmen there, who laughed at him.

"What a fool he is!" they jeered.

But some of them wondered: "Can Song Qing be a saint?"

When he heard this, he remarked: "I try to make money to keep my family. I am no saint. Still, those who think me a fool are also wrong."

By the time he had sold drugs for forty years he had burned scores of notes of hand, some belonging to men who had since become highly paid officials in charge of several districts; and now one after another they sent gifts to his house. So though many did not pay cash and hundreds never paid at all, this did not prevent him from growing rich. For Song Qing took a long view, and made a greater profit as a result, unlike those petty tradesmen who fly into a rage if they fail to get cash and shout abuse till they make themselves enemies. Such a way of doing business is most short-sighted. In fact, these men were real fools.

Song Qing, on the contrary, did very well and was by no means a fool, for he stuck to his own way until he was rich. Each day brought him more customers, and he supplied them all. Men in disgrace, whose own friends and relatives shunned them, were never rudely treated by Song Qing, but continued to get the best drugs. So when they were back in power they repaid him well. This shows his far-sightedness.

But I see the men of today flock to those in the sun and spurn those in the shade — few are Song Qing's equal. People speak contemptuously of "market friendship". Yet Song Qing was a tradesman in the market, and not many friends nowadays take such a long view regarding repayment as he. If they did, then many of those in sad straits would not be left to perish. So it seems this "market friendship" is very much needed!

Some may object: "Song Qing was no ordinary tradesman."

To this I answer: "Agreed. Though Song Qing kept a shop, he did not behave like a tradesman. Unfortunately many of those who call themselves gentlemen — the men in government offices and colleges — do act like tradesmen! It was not in the market-place alone that Song Qing stood out."

Camel Guo, the Tree Planter

NOBODY knows what Camel Guo's real name was. Because he was a hunchback with a hump like a camel's when he walked, his countrymen gave him this nickname.

"Very good!" said Camel when he heard it. "I shall use this."

So he dropped his former name and called himself Camel.

He lived in the district of Fengle, west of Chang'an, and his trade was tree-planting. All the rich men of Chang'an who loved gardens, and all the vendors of fruit, tried to hire him. For the trees he planted or transplanted always lived; indeed they flourished exceedingly and bore abundant fruit which ripened early. Though other gardeners watched him and copied him, not one of them did so well.

One day someone asked him his secret.

"I have no special skill," replied Camel Guo. "To get the best out of each tree I simply respect its nature. A tree's roots must have room to spread and must be evenly laid; the soil must be old and also firmly tamped down. Once a tree is planted you should not move it or fret about it, but go away without another glance. While planting it, treat it as you would your own child; but then leave it alone. For so it will remain whole and develop to the full. I simply refrain from injuring its growth; I cannot make it flourish. I merely keep from spoiling its fruit; I cannot make it fruitful or quick to ripen. Other gardeners are different. They crowd the roots together and use new soil, spreading either too much or too little; or if they avoid these mistakes, they handle the tree and worry about it too much, gazing at it by day and fingering it by night, coming back to it all the time. Some even scratch the bark to see whether it is still living, or tug at its roots to see whether they are firm; and so the tree withers away from day to day. Such men declare they love trees when in fact they are murdering them, and claim they are showing concern when in fact they are doing damage. This is how they fall short of me. But what more can I do?"

"Could your way be applied to the art of government?" asked the other.

"All I understand is planting trees," replied Camel. "Governing is not my line. Still, living here in the country I see the authorities issue order after order as if they had the people's welfare at heart; yet only harm comes of it. Day and night those officials come and shout: 'The magistrate orders you to get on with your ploughing! See that your planting is done! Get in your crops! Hurry up and card the silk! Look sharp and weave your thread! Bring up your children well! Feed your fowl and pigs!' They sound drums and clappers to summon the common people, and we go without both meals to entertain them; but if we have no time to ourselves, how can we thrive or live at peace? Instead, we waste away and are worn out. In this sense, governing men may be rather like planting trees."

The other man laughed.

"Wonderful!" he exclaimed. "I was asking how to grow trees, but here I have learned the way to govern men."

I record this as a warning for officials.

The Story of the Boy Ou Ji

THE people of Yue were so unfeeling that they looked upon their sons and daughters as merchandise, and used to sell them for a profit when they had lost their milk teeth. As if this were not enough, they would steal other people's children too and bind or chain them. Even men with beards, if too weak to resist, were carried away as slaves; and kidnapping was all too common. He who was lucky enough to reach manhood would catch those weaker than himself. And since this profited the Han officials, provided they got the slaves, they asked no questions. Thus the population of Yue kept decreasing, for few could avoid capture. It is strange, then, that Ou Ji, a boy of only eleven, managed to make good his escape.

This story was told me by Du Zhoushi, secretary of Gui Prefecture. Ou Ji was a cowherd in Liuzhou, who was watching his herd and gathering fuel when two brigands caught him. After tying his arms behind his back and gagging him, they set off with him to a market-town more than forty *li* away to sell him as a slave. The boy whimpered and trembled like any frightened child, and the brigands thought him easy prey. So having got drunk together, one of them went to the market while the other lay down, planting his sword in the ground. When Ou Ji saw the brigand was asleep, with his back to the sword the rubbed his bonds against the blade till he managed to cut through them. Then he killed the brigand with the sword and fled.

He had not gone far, however, when the other brigand came back and found him; and, in horror, the brigand prepared to kill him. But he quickly begged for mercy.

"Surely," he pleaded, "a slave shared by two men is not as good as a slave all to yourself. He treated me badly; but if you will spare my life and treat me kindly, I will do whatever you say."

After some thought the brigand said to himself: "It will pay me better to sell this boy than to kill him; and dividing what he fetches between two is not as good as keeping it all myself. Really it is fortunate that he killed the other fellow!"

He disposed of the corpse, and took the boy to the slave-broker. Once more Ou Ji was bound, this time more strongly. But in the middle of the night he wiggled up to the stove and set fire to his ropes to sever them. Even though he burned his hands, he did not falter. Then he drew the sword to kill the second brigand, and raised such a cry that the whole market was aroused.

"I am a son of the Ou family," he told the market people. "I ought not to be a slave, but two brigands kidnapped me. Now luckily I have killed them both. Report this to the authorities."

Then the head of the market told the magistrate, and the magistrate told the prefect, who summoned the boy. Seeing how small and gentle he looked, Yan Zheng, the prefect, was amazed. He offered him a small official post, but the boy declined; so he gave him some clothes instead, and sent him back under escort to his district, where all the kidnappers went in such fear of him that they dared not pass his door.

"This boy is two years younger than Qin Wuyang,"* they said. "But he has already killed two bold men. We had better keep out of his way."

---

* A boy of the kingdom of Yan during the Warring States Period (403-221 B.C.), who killed a man at the age of thirteen.

The Story of a Master-Builder

My brother-in-law Pei lives in Guangde Lane. Once a master-builder knocked at his door and asked to rent a corner of the house. As gear he had compasses, a ruler, square, marking-line and ink, but in his room he kept no grindstone or chisel.

When asked what skills he had he said, "I am good at estimating the materials needed for building. When I design a structure, I calculate its measurements and decide what should be round, square, long or short, then give instructions to the various workmen. Without me they could not build it. So when I draw my pay from the government I get three times as much as the other workmen, and when I work for a private family more than half the fee is mine."

Another day when I went to his room, I saw that one leg of his bed was broken but he was unable to repair it and said he would find another workman to do it. I was very amused, considering him a useless fellow who was out only for money.

Later the city magistrate wanted to have his office repaired, and I went there. All sorts of building material had been assembled there and all kinds of workmen, some with axes, some with choppers, others with saws. They stood in a semi-circle facing the master-builder in the middle, a ruler in his left hand, a stick in his right. Having estimated the strength needed to support the beams and the roof and that of the timber, he waved his stick saying, "Cut here." As one workman with an axe ran to the right, he pointed at the other side and said, "Saw it off here." Thereupon a workman with a saw ran to the left. Then some hewed wood, others whittled it, all watching his expression and waiting for his orders, not daring to make any decisions themselves. If anyone bungled, he angrily dismissed him and the man dared not show displeasure.

He made a drawing of the building on the wall which, though only about a foot square, gave all the details. When it was completed according to this plan, nothing was a fraction out. Then he wrote on the ridge-pole the year, month and day of the construction and signed his own name, omitting those of the men who had done the job. I looked round in amazement, only then realizing how great was his skill.

With a sigh I wondered: Has he given up manual skills to concentrate on using his mind and grasping the overall plan? I have heard that those who toil with their minds make others work for them, while those who toil with their hands work for others and serve those who use their minds. This must be one who toils with his mind. Men with skill use their skill while men with intelligence make plans. This is an intelligent man, a worthy model for the prime minister who helps his sovereign rule an empire, for their tasks are very similar.

One who rules an empire has his roots in the people. Those who toil are the slaves and village heads, above them are the gentry, high and low, and above them the knights, ministers and nobles. They are divided into six ministries or a hundred different professions. Then within the Four Seas there are barons commanding different regions, and each province has its governor, each district its magistrate, all of whom assist in the work of government; under them are the officers, and under the local officers are the bailiffs and runners, each with his task, just as workmen all do their individual jobs to earn their keep. Then the man who acts as the prime minister helps the emperor to rule over them all, giving orders, working out the general plan, making modifications and laying down rules to regulate them, just as a master-builder uses his ruler, square, marking-line and ink to decide on the system of work.

The prime minister selects men from all parts of the empire and settles them in the tasks for which they are suited, so that all the subjects live and work in peace and contentment. From the city he gains understanding of the countryside, from the countryside of the principalities, from the principalities of the whole empire. He can examine all things near and far, big and small, by referring to his plan, just as the master-builder brings a building to completion on the basis of the drawing on the wall. He promotes men of ability and lets them work according to their own bent, so that they feel indebted to no one; he dismisses men who are incapable, and they dare not show displeasure. He makes no boast of his own ability and seeks no personal fame, does not interfere with minor tasks or infringe on the rights of his officers, but spends all his time discussing affairs of state with men of talent. This is like the master-builder's skill in making use of all his workmen and not boasting of his own ability. By so doing he succeeds as a prime minister and can bring order to all the principalities. Then the people of the whole empire look up to him and credit the success to him, while posterity will follow in his footsteps and praise him as an able prime minister.

When men speak of the good government of the Shang and Zhou dynasties, they attribute this to such men as Yi Yin, Fu Yue, the Duke of Zhou and the Duke of Shao, while all those doing the routine tasks are not mentioned in the records, just as the master-builder signs his name on the construction, omitting those of the workmen.

The art of the prime minister is indeed great. Only those who have mastered it can be called prime ministers, not those who do not understand the essential plan. Such men consider assiduity their duty and paper-work all important. They boast of their ability and seek personal fame, attend to minor affairs and infringe on the rights of their officers. They gloat in their office over all the routine work they have arrogated to themselves, but neglect important affairs and plans for the future. These are men who do not know the right way to govern. Like a master-builder unable to use the marking-line, ink, compasses, ruler and square, they take over the workmen's axes, choppers and saws to show their skill, but can get no work done. So finally they fail and achieve nothing. Such behaviour is certainly ridiculous.

Some may ask: What if the man who has commissioned the house wants to show his own intelligence and obstructs the master-builder's plan, taking the management out of his hands and adopting counter-plans? Although the result is failure, this is not the master-builder's fault but that of his employer.

My answer to this is no. For there are the marking-line, ink, ruler and square. If something should be high, one cannot force it to be low; if something should be narrow, one cannot extend it. If the plan is followed the building will stand firm; otherwise it will collapse. If the owner prefers it not to stand firm but collapse, then the master-builder should roll up his plan, keep his ideas to himself and leave, without compromising. Such a man is a good master-builder. If he hankers after profit and cannot bear to give up the work, but abandons the right measurements and design and compromises, so that later the beams buckle and the house collapses, how can he claim that it is not his fault? Impossible!

In the belief that a master-builder's way is similar to that of a prime minister, I have written this down as a record. In the old days a master-builder was called a contractor; now we call such a man a supervisor or foreman. The one I came across was named Yang. I will not give his personal name.

Dung-Beetles

DUNG-beetles like to carry loads. They pick up whatever lies in their path, raising their heads to carry it; and refuse to give up however heavy their load and however exhausted they are. Moreover, since their backs are abrasive, things piled on them will not slip off. So at last they stumble, fall, and cannot get up. Sometimes men take pity on them and remove their burden; but they pick it up again as soon as they can crawl on. They like climbing too, and press forward with all their might till they fall dead.

There are people today in the world who are fond of gain and will let slip no chance to enrich themselves, never thinking that this wealth may prove a burden. Their one fear is that they may not amass enough. When they grow careless and stumble, they may be demoted, banished or involved in trouble; yet as soon as they struggle to their feet they start again, scheming each day to better their position and procure a larger salary, till their greed for more gain brings them to the brink of ruin. They never reflect upon their previous setbacks. Though these seem stout fellows and are known as "men", they have no more intelligence than little beetles. How pathetic this is!

Three Fables

I have always disliked those men of today who, blind to their own shortcomings, take advantage of circumstances or powerful protectors to lord it over others, bragging of their skill and seizing every chance to swagger. Such bullies always come to grief in the end. I shall therefore relate three cautionary tales I have heard about a deer, a donkey and some rats, which remind me of such men.

The Deer of Linjiang

A man of Linjiang* caught a fawn and decided to keep it. But when he took it home, all his dogs bounded over drooling and wagging their tails. He angrily called them to heel. Every day after that he carried the fawn to the dogs to accustom them to it and teach them not to hurt it. And by degrees he allowed them to play together.

As time went by, all his dogs did as he wished. The fawn grew up and forgot it was a deer, thinking dogs were its true friends. It would butt them, lie down beside them, and make quite free with them. And the dogs, out of fear of their master, played up to it. From time to time, though, they would lick their chaps.

* Present-day Qingjiang County in Jiangxi Province.

When three years had passed, the deer went out of the gate. Seeing many dogs from elsewhere on the road, it ran over to play with them. But the sight of it threw these strange dogs into a frenzy. They fell on the deer and devoured it, scattering its remains on the ground. And so the deer perished without understanding the reason.

The Donkey of Guizhou

THERE were no donkeys in Guizhou until someone officious took one there by boat; but finding no use for it he set it loose in the hills. A tiger who saw this monstrous looking beast thought it must be divine. It first surveyed the donkey from under cover, then ventured a little nearer, still keeping a respectful distance however.

One day the donkey brayed. The tiger took fright and fled for fear of being bitten, in utter terror. But it came back for another look, and decided this creature was not so formidable after all. Then growing used to the braying it drew nearer, though it still dared not attack. Coming nearer still, it began to take liberties, shoving, jostling, and charging roughly, till the donkey lost its temper and kicked out.

"So that's all it can do!" thought the tiger jubilantly.

Then it leapt on the donkey and sank its teeth into it, severing its throat and devouring it before going on its way.

Poor donkey! Its size made it look powerful, and its bray made it sound redoubtable. Had it not shown all it was capable of, the tiger fierce as it was might not have dared to attack. But such, alas, was the donkey's untimely end!

The Rats of Yongzhou

A certain householder in Yongzhou had a dread of unlucky days and observed strict taboos. Because he was born in the year of the Rat,* he considered rats as holy. This being the case, he would keep no cat or dog and forbade his servants to catch rats. Unchecked, they had the run of his store-rooms and kitchen.

As news of this spread among rats, more and more of them flocked to his house, where they could eat their fill with nothing to fear. They broke all the household utensils and gnawed through all the clothes on the hangers. The household had to make do with the food they left over. Processions of rats mingled freely with men in broad daylight, and at night they made such a din by gnawing things up and fighting that no one could sleep. Still the inmates of the house put up with them.

After some years this family left and another household moved in, but the rats carried on as before.

"These are creatures of darkness," said the newcomers, "but now they are running riot. Why were they allowed to get out of hand like this?"

They borrowed five or six cats, closed all the doors, removed the tiles from the roof and poured water down all the holes, hiring men to help them catch the rats. Soon a mound of dead rats was piled up in a corner, and the place stank for several months.

---

* The ancient Chinese believed that different years were governed by different animal deities.

This is a lesson for those who think they can fill their bellies for ever at the expense of others with nothing to fear.

The Whip

A man was selling whips in the market. When asked the price, though his whips were worth fifty cash only, he demanded fifty thousand. If offered fifty, he held his stomach and laughed; if offered five hundred, he frowned; if offered five thousand, he flew into a rage. He must have fifty thousand.

One day a rich man's son went to the market to buy a whip, and paid this fellow fifty thousand for one. He brought it out to show me. The head was knotted and gnarled, the stock was warped and crooked, the grain did not run through the whole, and the nodes were rotten and bare of ornament. When I pinched it my nail sank right in, and when I lifted it it was light as air.

"Why did you pay fifty thousand for this?" I asked.

"I like this yellow colour and glossy sheen," he replied. "Besides, that was the price asked."

I told his servant to wash it with hot water, and at once it turned withered and grey; for the yellow colour was a dye, and the sheen was caused by beeswax.

The rich man was disappointed; nevertheless he kept the whip for three years. Then one day he went to the eastern suburb to race with some friends by Changle Slope. When the horses started kicking and he lashed out at them, his whip broke into fragments; but the horses went on kicking, and he fell and injured himself. Upon looking inside the whip, he found it hollow, of a texture most like mud, without any substance.

Now there are men with a specious appearance and honeyed words, who try to sell their skill to the government. If others make a mistake and think better of them than they deserve, they are very pleased; but if rightly judged they grow angry, and demand: "Why am I not made a minister?" Many of them, indeed, hold high positions. In quiet times they may go unscathed for three years or more; but as soon as trouble starts and they are sent to responsible posts to take charge, it is no use expecting these hollow, shoddy whips to prove effective. They are bound to break, and then people will be thrown and injured.

Fool's Stream

NORTH of the River Guan is a stream which flows eastwards into the River Xiao. Some say this stream is called Ran because a family named Ran once lived there; others say it was so called because its water can be used for dyeing. * After I was punished for my folly by being exiled to the bank of the Xiao, I fell in love with this stream and followed it for two or three *li* until I came to its most delightful spot, then settled down there. In ancient times there used to be a Fool's Valley. Now that I was staying by this stream, the name of which had not yet been determined but

---

* The Chinese word for "dye" is also pronounced "ran".

was still being disputed by the local people, I had to give it a name. So I renamed it Fool's Stream.

Beside Fool's Stream I bought a hillock, and called it Fool's Mound. Sixty paces northeast I discovered a fountain, which I also purchased and named Fool's Fountain. Fool's Fountain, which has its source higher up, has six outlets on the flat ground at the foot of this hillock. These brooklets join and wind southwards to Fool's Ditch. I had earth and stones carried over to dam the narrowest part of the ditch to form Fool's Pond. East of Fool's Pond stands Fool's Hall, with Fool's Pavilion to its south. In the middle of the pool is Fool's Islet, with an abundance of fine trees and curious rocks. These are all rare sights, but because of me they have been given a bad name.

Since water is appreciated by all intelligent men, * why did I give this stream the bad name Fool's Stream? Because it flows through low ground, it cannot be used to irrigate fields; and because it runs swiftly and is filled with boulders, large boats cannot navigate it. Moreover, since it is out of the way, shallow and narrow, dragons must scorn to make clouds and rain of its water; hence it does no good to men. This is just like my own case, and therefore I am not wrong to call it Fool's Stream.

Ning Wuzi** posed as a fool when his state was badly governed — a case of a wise man turning into a fool. Yan Zi*** seemed a fool because he never contradicted anyone — a case of a judicious man appearing like a fool. These were not real fools. Now I live

---

* A quotation from the *Analects*: "The intelligent man appreciates water."
** A native of the state of Wei, who lived in the seventh century B.C.
*** The favourite disciple of Confucius.

in an age of good rule, but I acted counter to reason and made mistakes in my work; so there can be no greater fool than I. This being so, no one in the world can dispute my ownership of this stream: I can keep it to myself and name it as I please.

Though this stream does no good to men, it reflects all things clearly, being limpid and transparent, and tinkles merrily; so a fool is happy to linger here, and cannot bear to go away. Though I am unfitted for worldly affairs, I find great comfort in writing, touching upon all subjects, embracing all forms, and avoiding nothing. When I sing my foolish songs about Fool's Stream, we seem to merge with no discord into one, blending into the infinity of space, growing utterly tranquil and divested of self. Thus I wrote "Eight Poems on the Fool", and had them inscribed on a rock beside the stream.

A Drinking Game

AFTER buying my hillock I spent the first day weeding it and the second cleaning it up, then gave a drinking party on the rocks by the stream.

These rocks, as I have set down elsewhere, look like cattle being watered. Sitting apart on them, we first filled our cups and set them afloat for others to take up and drink. Then we made this rule: when it was someone's turn to drink, he must throw three bamboo slips about ten inches long upstream; if the slips were neither caught up by an eddy, blocked by a boulder nor sunk, he need not drink. But each time one of these things happened, he must drain a cup.

So we started throwing the slips. They whirled around, dancing and leaping in the current, now quick, now slow, some skimming along, some stopping. And we all leaned forward to watch, clapping and cheering them on. Suddenly one would fly past in safety; thus some drank one cup only, others two.

Among the guests was a man called Lou Tunan. His first slip was caught in an eddy, his second was blocked and his third sank; so he was the only one to drain all three cups. We roared with laughter and were very merry.

I have dyspepsia and cannot drink, but that day I was drunk. Then we modified the rules, and went on till night without thinking of going home.

I have heard that when the ancients drank wine, some bowed and deferred to each other punctiliously; some shouted and danced in complete abandon; some stripped off their clothes to show unconventionality; some made music for the sake of harmony; some drank fast in large groups in order to be convivial.

Our drinking, though, is different. It is decorous without formality, unconstrained without noise, informal without nakedness, harmonious without music, convivial without a crowd. Simple yet sociable, free and easy yet polite, leisurely yet dignified, it is an excellent accompaniment for the enjoyment of nature and fit relaxation for gentlemen. So I record this for those who come after us.

The Thatched Pavilion on Matui Mountain

IN the tenth month, a new pavilion was built on the south side of Matui Mountain. With a high mount at its back, it has no ornamental pillars, intricate carvings or painted ceiling; the beams are unpolished, the thatch untrimmed, and it has no walls. White clouds serving as its fence, green hills as its screen, set off its frugality.

This mountain looms over a vast expanse of green and soars up to the clouds, stretching for dozens of miles with its tail curled up in the wilderness and its head dipping into a big stream. All the other hills converge to pay homage to it like a cluster of stars. Verdant green and fantastically shaped, it resembles a magnificent embroidered tapestry. Heaven has indeed concentrated beauty here, although this is such a remote border region. However, since this is an uncultivated area and the people have barbarous customs, even King Mu of the Zhou Dynasty never came here with his fine horses, nor did the poet Xie Lingyun ever climb up here in his clogs; thus the mountain paths were desolate and people were deterred from trying to climb it.

In the sixth year of Yuanhe (A. D. 811), my second brother was assigned to this district by the governor. As his virtue spread, trust in him grew and he got on well with the people. Since they were in harmony, he could enjoy more leisure when his official duties were done, and he often came to this mountain to enjoy the superb scenery; then he decided to build this wooden pavilion which in no time was completed. When there was no wind or rain and the sky was clear and bright, putting on a peaked cap and a deer-skin coat he would climb this mountain with five or six young brothers and friends, then play the lyre and follow with his eyes the clouds returning to the valleys. As the fresh air of the west hills filled his lapel and sleeves, all the myriad things in nature seemed to be within his grasp.

Now a beauty spot is only made manifest when men praise it: if the Orchid Pavilion had not had Wang Xizhi, its clear brook and luxuriant bamboos would have gone unrecognized in the empty hills. As this pavilion stands in the mountains of the south, this beauty spot is rarely visited, and did I not record its construction this fine sight would remain unknown. Hence I have made this record.

The New Hall of Prefect Wei of Yongzhou

TO make valleys, cliffs and pools in a city, mountain rocks have to be carted there, chasms dug, many difficulties and obstacles overcome, and a great deal of manpower exhausted. Even then one cannot create a natural scene. However, if one avoids the artificial, laying out the grounds according to the terrain and preserving the natural surroundings, what has proved so difficult already takes shape there.

Yongzhou lies at the foot of the Jiuyi Mountains. Those who first opened up this district built the city round the hills, with rocks left hidden in the grasses and streams concealed by the roads. As snakes coiled through the undergrowth in which weasels roamed, while fine trees and rank vegetation contended together, it was known as a garbage dump.

After Prefect Wei had been here for over a month and ordered his affairs so that he had leisure, his interest was attracted to this place. First he ordered it to be weeded and had the roads repaired. Earth was piled up into mounds and the streams were dredged so that the water flowed clear. After the brambles had been burnt and the streams channelled, many wonderful sights appeared. The muddy water turned clear, fine plants took the place of the weeds. When you look at the vegetation now, it is all graceful and luxuriant; when you view the streams, they are gentle and meandering; grotesque rocks loom on every side, some in rows or like men kneeling, some erect and others prostrate, with intricate crevices and caves as well as mounts rearing up as if in anger.

Prefect Wei had this hall built then for sightseers. At its foot, all manner of objects display themselves to contribute to the view. Beyond lie hills, high plains and forests, some clearly visible and others hidden, with a green stretch of grassland which merges with the blue sky at the horizon, and all these sights can be seen from the watch-tower. He invited guests to this hall to feast and take pleasure.

Congratulating him they said, "From what you have accomplished, sir, we see your ideal. You want to create beauty befitting the terrain; this surely means that you want to rule according to local customs. You select what is beautiful among what is ugly; this surely means that you want to get rid of despots and help the good. You dredge muddy streams to make them flow clear; this surely means that you want to dimiss corrupt officials and appoint honest men. You have built this hall on a height to command a view of the distance; this surely means that you want all local households to be familiar with your instructions. In this case, building this hall does not merely mean making suitable use of the flora, rocks and streams to create a beauty spot with hills, plains and forests, but through this small example you want your successors to grasp what is important."

So I asked to have this record inscribed on a stone and set at the northwest corner, as an example for future prefects.

My First Visit to the Western Hill

AFTER I was degraded I lived a most uneasy life in this district. I filled in my time with long walks and aimless rambles, climbed hills every day with my men, or explored deep woods and winding streams, visiting hidden springs and curious rocks no matter how distant. Once there, we would sit on the grass and pour out wine, to fall asleep when drunk resting our heads on each other while my dreams followed my roving fancy. Then, upon waking, we would rise and walk back. I thought at that time I knew all the strange sights in this district, but I had no conception of the wonders of the Western Hill.

On the twenty-eighth of the ninth month this year, as I was sitting in the west pavilion of Fahua Monastery and looking towards the Western Hill, I began to be struck by its singularity. I ordered my servants to ferry me across the River Xiang; then we followed the Ran to its source, cutting down the brambles and burning the rushes on our way till we reached the summit of the hill.

After struggling to the top we squatted down to rest. The fields of several districts lay spread below my seat. There were undulating slopes with gaps and hollows, as well as mounds and burrows. A thousand *li* appeared like one foot or one inch, so compact that nothing escaped our sight. Encompassed by white clouds and azure sky, the hill merged with them into one single whole.

Then I realized that this was no common hill. I felt I was mingling freely with the boundless expanse of heaven, and lost myself in the infinity of nature. In utter content I filled my cup and got drunk, unaware that the sun had set. Dark night came from afar and soon nothing could be seen, yet still I was loath to leave; for my heart seemed to have ceased beating and I felt released from my body to blend with the myriad forms of created things. I knew then that I had never enjoyed an excursion before — this was my first such experience.

So I am writing this record in the fourth year of Yuanhe. *

---

* A.D. 809.

Brazier Lake

BRAZIER Lake lies west of the Western Hill. Its source is the Ran which plunges south till, stopped by a mountain boulder, it veers east and races along, pounding against the bank, till now it has eaten away a large tract of land, channelling out the centre down to impermeable rock. After foaming into a whirlpool, it flows slowly into ten *mu* of calm, clear water, embowered with trees and with fountains cascading into it.

The man who lived above this lake saw how often I visited it. One day he knocked at my door, and told me that because he could not pay his taxes and was deep in debt he had made a clearing in the hills and was moving away. He wanted to sell his property by the lake to try to tide himself over.

I fell in with this gladly. Then I rebuilt his pavilion, extended his balustered walks, and made the fountain there fall into the pool from a height with a deep echoing sound. So now no better spot can be found for enjoying the moon in mid-autumn, for here you can see the sublimity of the sky, the infinity of space. And thanks to this lake I can rest content in these wild parts and forget my home!

The Knoll West of Brazier Lake

EIGHT days after my discovery of the Western Hill, two hundred paces northwest from the mouth of that valley, I hit upon

Brazier Lake.

Twenty-five paces further west a deep rapid had been dammed to make a fish-pond, and beside this rose a knoll, grown over with bamboos and other trees. It had countless rocks of fantastic shapes projecting from the ground: here a chain of boulders like cattle trooping down to be watered, there crags rising sheer like bears toiling up the hill. The entire knoll covered less than one *mu* — you could fence in the whole of it easily.

I asked who the owner was.

"It belongs to the Tang family," I was told. "They have no use for it, but haven't been able to sell it."

I asked the price.

"Only four hundred cash," was the answer.

Then I could not resist buying it. Li Shenyuan and Yuan Keji, who were with me at the time, were in raptures at such unexpected good fortune. We fetched tools to mow the rank weeds and cut the dead wood, and burnt them in a blazing fire. Then the good trees and fine bamboos appeared to advantage, and the strange shaped rocks stood out. From here you have a view of high hills, floating clouds and flowing streams, while beasts and birds frolic below, displaying themselves merrily. When you lie on a mat, cool greenery rests your eyes, running water soothes your ear, the great void revives your spirit, and the utter quietness refreshes your heart. Thus in less than ten days I have found two remarkable places, which not even the venturesome scholars of old appear to have visited.

Ah, if such natural beauty as this knoll possesses were put near the capital, the lovers of pleasure trips there would jostle each other in their eagerness to buy, offering an extra thousand each day — to no purpose. But in these forsaken parts, the peasants and fishermen pass it by, setting no store by it; and priced at four hundred cash, for years it remained unsold. So now — such is fate! — Shenyuan, Keji and I are the only ones who enjoy it!

I inscribe this on stone to congratulate this knoll on having found an owner.

The Small Tarn West of the Knoll

A hundred and twenty paces west of the knoll, across the bamboos and bushes I heard with delight a gurgling like the sound made by jade bracelets. So I cut a path through the bamboos till I came upon a small pool of clear water. The bottom was of rock and a spring gushed out from the boulders near the bank. Rocks formed little islets and crags, overhung by green trees and vines which were growing in great profusion. There were about a hundred fish in the tarn, and they seemed to be gliding through empty space without support. In the sunlight which reached the bottom, casting shadows over the rocks, the fish would stay for a while motionless then suddenly dart far away. They scudded to and fro, as if sharing the visitors' delight.

Looking southwest in the chequered sunlight at the jagged, serpentine shore, you could not see the whole.

I sat by this tarn, with bamboos and trees all around me, in utter silence and solitude. The seclusion and quiet cast a chill over me; and the scene was one of such purity that I could not stay there long. So I marked the spot and left.

With me were Wu Wuling, Gong You, and my brother Zong-xuan. And two of the Cui boys, Shuji and Fengyi, had accompanied us to help us.

Yuan Family Ghyll

TEN *li* southwest of the Ran by boat are five fine sights, of which Brazier Lake is the best. West of the mouth of the Ran by land are eight or nine fine sights, of which the Western Hill is the best. Southeast of Chaoyang Cliff by boat to the River Wu are three fine sights, of which Yuan Family Ghyll is the best. These quiet scenes are the beauty spots of Yongzhou.

According to the local dialect, there is a special word, ghyll, for water-that-runs-in-the-opposite-direction-from-the-main-stream. Yuan Family Ghyll flows into Nanguan in its upper reaches, and further down into Hundred Families Creek. Here you find twin islets, brooks, clear pools and shallows; and the ghyll winds past flat, dark rocks and towering, foam-white crags. Just as your boat seems to reach the end, a new vista opens up. There are small islands in the water covered with magnificent boulders and green foliage which remains luxuriant summer and winter a-like. The caves on either side are strewn with white pebbles. The trees are mostly maple, cedar, nanmu, yellow box, oak, camphor-laurel or pumelo. The chief flowers are orchids and irises. And a strange plant resembling acacia, except that it is a creeper, grows on all the rocks in the stream. When a wind blows down from the surrounding mountains, the great trees are buffeted and the flowers toss their heads in a flurry of crimson and green, scattering pungent fragrance. Waves eddy and whirl, and fill every cleft in the rocks, while the bayonet-leafed iris and orchid quiver and bend. Such is the pageant of the seasons, passing my powers of description.

Since the people of Yongzhou did not know of this place, after finding it I could not keep it to myself, but spread its fame abroad. The land through which it runs has belonged for generations to a family called Yuan, hence the name — Yuan Family Ghyll.

The Rocky Trough

LESS than a hundred paces southwest from the ghyll, I found a rocky trough. A plank had been thrown across it. A spring bubbles out from the stones there, now gurgling merrily, now murmuring softly. This trough measures one to two feet across and about ten paces in length. The brook, coming to a great boulder, passes under it.

Crossing this boulder, I came to a grotto overgrown with sweet flags and with green moss all around.

There the brook turns west and dips sideways under a cliff, cascading northward into a little pool. This pool, less than a hundred feet around, is clear and deep and has many white fish in it.

Northward the brook winds on and on, as if it will never end, but finally enters the ghyll.

By the trough are fantastic rocks, gnarled trees, strange flowers, and graceful young bamboos. Several men can sit there at a time to rest. When the wind strikes the hill top, an echo is heard in the valley. The scene is tranquil, and sound travels far.

After acquiring this property from the prefect, I cleared the dead wood and leaves and made a bonfire of them, then removed some of the earth and stones from the trough so that the water should flow more freely. It seemed a pity that no record had been made of this place, so I wrote a detailed account and left it with the local people to inscribe on the south of the boulder. In this way, sightseers after us will find this spot easily.

On the eighth day of the first month of the seventh year of Yuanhe, * I cleared the way from the trough to the great boulder. But not till the nineteenth of the tenth month, when I crossed the boulder and found the grotto and pool, did I discover the full beauty of the trough.

The Rocky Gorge

AFTER exploring the trough I struck northwest from the bridge down the north side of the hill, to where another bridge has been made. The water here is one third wider than at the trough. And from bank to bank the brook is paved with rock which resembles in turn a couch, a hall, a banqueting table, or an inner chamber. The water flows smoothly over, with ripples like patterned silk

* A.D. 812.

and a sound like the strumming of a lyre. I tucked up my clothes and went barefoot, breaking off bamboos, sweeping away dead leaves and clearing the rotten wood, so that now eighteen or nineteen people can recline on hammocks here. The waves eddy and gurgle beneath these hammocks, which are shaded by trees with green plumage and rocks with dragon scales. What men of old knew such enjoyment as this? Will later generations tread in my footsteps? My pleasure that day was as great as when I discovered the trough.

From Yuan Family Ghyll you come first to the trough, then to this gorge. From Hundred Families Creek you come first to the gorge, then to the trough.

The only accessible part of the gorge is southeast of Stone Town Village, where there are several delightful spots. Further up, the high hills and dark forests grow steep and impenetrable, and the narrow paths are difficult to follow.

Stone Town Mount

THE road north from the Western Hill, down across Yellow Rush Peak, leads to two paths. One strikes west, but I found nothing of interest there. The other veers northeast, and is stopped in less than four hundred feet by a stream with a cairn beside it to serve as a boundary. The rocks above look like a city wall, and the gate on one side like a gate into a fort. It is very dark within. I threw in a pebble, which fell with a splash, a clear echo ringing after it for some time. You can climb the mount skirting these rocks, and once at the top can see far into the distance. Although there is no soil, the fine trees and slender bamboos which grow there are more curiously shaped and firmly rooted than most. Some are high, some low; some grow in clumps, and others stand apart as if planted by a skilful hand.

Indeed, I have long been curious to know whether or not a Creator exists; and this sight made me feel that there must surely be one. It seems strange, though, that such wonders are set not in the heart of the country but in barbarous regions like this, where hundreds of years may pass before anyone comes along to appreciate them. This is labour in vain, which hardly befits a god, so perhaps there is none after all!

Some say, "This is done to comfort good men who are sent here in disgrace."

Others say, "This climate does not produce great men, but only freaks of nature. That is why there are few men south of Chu,* but many rocks."

I do not hold, however, with either view.

---

* A region corresponding roughly to what is now Hunan Province.

LI HE

Li He (790-816) was born to a family of declining fortunes distantly related to the royal house. During his short lifetime he produced a body of poetry which, in its haunting and morbid imagery, has provoked frequent comparisons with Baudelaire and the French Symbolists. His work was sufficiently unorthodox to have been excluded from the majority of Tang anthologies. Li exhibited a fondness for unusual diction and rhyme schemes and his eerie and dramatic images were often drawn from folk religion and mythology. His work has had a considerable influence on later poets.

Li Ping's Harp

SILK strings from Wu, plane wood from Shu, *
Music that swells the vaulted autumn sky!
On lonely hills the clouds freeze and are still,
The river nymphs** weep in their bamboo grove
And the white virgin*** aches with envy
When Li Ping in the Middle Kingdom starts to play.
Jade shattered in the mountain, the cry of the phoenix,
Dewy tears of lotus, the chuckle of fragrant orchids;
This music melts the icy light at the twelve imperial gates.
These strings move the Purple Emperor**** himself;
And where Nü Wa patched the sky with molten rock
It cracks, startling heaven, hastening the autumn rain.
I dream that on holy mountain he teaches a witch to play
While old fish leap in the waves, gaunt dragons dance;
The man in the moon leans, sleepless, against his cassia
    tree,
And the slanting steps of dew spray the frosty hare.

---

* The lower Yangtse Valley (Wu) was famed for its silk, and Sichuan (Shu) for its
  fine wood.
** The wives of the legendary sage king Shun, who grieved because he died in exile.
*** The legendary Yellow Emperor's daughter, credited with the invention of the
  harp.
**** The Emperor of Heaven in Taoist legend.

The Governor of Yanmen

BLACK clouds bear down upon the tottering town,
Mail glints like golden fish-scales in the sun,
Bugling invests the sky with autumn splendour
As crimson forts freeze in the purple dusk;
Red flags half furled withdraw to the River Yi,
Our drums roll faint, muffled in heavy frost,
And to repay honour conferred from the golden dais,*
I draw my Jade Dragon Sword to die for my lord!

A Dream of Heaven

THE hoary hare and frosty toad have washed the sky with
    tears,**
Half open the cloudy pavilion, its wall slanting white,
And the jade wheel grinding dew wets its orb of light;
Wearing phoenix pendants they meet on a path sweet with
    cassia,
Those to whom the magic isles below are but yellow dust and
    clear water;
A thousand years flash by like galloping horses,

---

  * The dais from which the governor received his appointment from the emperor.
  ** Legend has it that a hare and toad lived in the moon, described as a pavilion of
clouds or a jade wheel.

The nine continents far away seem nine wisps of smoke, *
The vast ocean no more than water spilled from a cup.

Song of the Bronze Statue

In the eighth month of the first year of the Qing Long era, during the reign of Emperor Ming of Wei, the court ordered a palace officer to ride west and bring back the gilded bronze figure of an immortal holding a disc to catch dew made in the reign of Emperor Wu of Han, in order to set it up in the front court. When the palace officer removed the disc and took the statue to his carriage, the bronze figure shed tears. So Li Changji, descended from a prince of the House of Tang, made this song.

GONE that emperor of Maoling,
Rider through the autumn wind,
Whose horse neighs at night
And has passed without trace by dawn.
The fragrance of autumn lingers still
On those cassia trees by painted galleries,
But on every palace hall the green moss grows.
As Wei's envoy sets out to drive a thousand *li*
The keen wind at the East Gate stings the statue's eyes...

From the ruined palace he brings nothing forth

---

* Referring to the nine regions of China in old maps.

But the moon-shaped disc of Han,

True to his lord, he sheds leaden tears,

And withered orchids by the Xianyang Road

See the traveller on his way.

Ah, if Heaven had a feeling heart, it too must grow old!

He bears the disc off alone

By the light of a desolate moon,

The town far behind him, muted its lapping waves.

The Old Man Quarrying Jade

QUARRYING, quarrying,

For green translucent jade

To make pendants for beautiful ladies,

The old man goes cold and hungry

And the dragon chafes in his pool,

For the once clear waters of the Lan are troubled. *

On rainy nights on the hill he feeds on acorns,

His tears endless as the nightingale's anguished song;

The Lan is surfeited with human lives,

Haunted by ghosts of the drowned for long centuries.

Wind and rain shriek through the cypress trees on the slope,

Ropes stretch green and sinuous down to the bed of the
   pool;

---

* The Lan was a stream at Lantian near Chang'an, in the bed of which good jade
was found.

He thinks of his little ones in the poor, cold hut,
When on the steps leading up to the ruined terrace
He sees the vine called Heart-break.

The Toast

A cup of wine for a vagabond:
My host wishes me a long life.
"Zhufu Yan * was hard put to it to return from the west,
While his family snapped the willows at their gate,
So long did they watch for him.
And Ma Zhou, ** living as a protégé at Xinfeng,
Thought he would go unrecognized for ever;
But a couple of lines he wrote on a report
Went straight to the throne and won him imperial
    favour..."
I fear my spirit has strayed beyond recall,
Yet one crow of the cock will flood the world with light;
A young man should aspire to reach for the sky,
Who will care for one who sits in the cold and sighs?

---

  * A scholar of Qi who went to Chang'an and was finally recommended to Emperor
    Wu of the Han Dynasty so that he became a high official.

 ** A poor scholar in the Tang Dynasty. He presented a memorandum to Emperor
    Taizong, who made him an imperial censor.

Heigh-ho!

HEIGH-HO, singing rends my clothes!
Heigh-ho, singing thins my white hair!
Kept from the presence of the emperor,
Day and night consumed with longing,
I quench my thirst with wine from the pot
And stay my hunger with millet from the fields,
Lonely as May slips by
Though all is green for a thousand *li* around.
The mountain looms clear at night,
The bright moon shining down to its foot,
But when I grope through boulders towards that light
It floats high above the peak,
And debarred from approaching
I sing as my hair turns white.

A Satire

NO pearls left in Hepu,
No oranges in Longzhou!
It seems the Creator himself is powerless
To meet all the demands of the governor!
The women of the south have not started to weave,
Th silkworms are still curling on the leaves.
When up gallops the magistrate,

Grim-faced, with curled purple beard,
Displaying a square placard,
On the placard a written order.
"If you had not angered the governor,
Would I have come to your house?"
The woman curtseys to the magistrate.
"The mulberry leaves are still small,
Not until the end of spring
Can I set my loom whirring."
While she pleads with him
Her sister-in-law cooks a meal;
Barely has the magistrate bolted the food and left
When the bailiff is in the hall.

The Tower by the River

THE stream before her tower flows to Jiangling,*
A monsoon blows, the lotus is in bloom,
And dressing her hair at dawn she tells the south wind:
"Coming back with full sail
Would take him no more than a day."
Alligators weep by the bank in mizzling rain,
A fresh blue linen sign hangs before the inn,
The choppy waves have white crests, the clouds hang low,
This is the season to send him a cape for showers.

---

* Then an important trading centre in the upper reaches of the Yangtse.

New wine mutters in the press but still tastes thin,
The whole South Lake is mirror-bright;
As she gazes, her thoughts already far away,
Her maid draws back the screen and distant hills can be
  seen.

Song of the Sorceress

NOW sinks the sun behind the western hills,
The eastern hills grow dim,
And horses lashed by whirlwinds
Trample the clouds;
Plain pipes and painted strings
Make a medley of music
And she dances with rustling skirts
Through the autumn dust.
Cassia leaves swept by the wind
Let fall their seeds,
Dark hyenas weep tears of blood,
Foxes shiver and die;
The gaudy, gold-tailed dragon
On crumbling wall
Is ridden by rain-makers
To the autumn pool;
The owl in its hundredth year
Is transformed into a spirit of the wood,
And as it hoots with laughter
Green flames spring up from its nest.

A Drinking Song

RICH amber brims the crystal cup,
Red pearls drip from the little wine-press,
The jade fat of roasted dragon and phoenix sizzles,
And silken tapestries hold wafted fragrance...
Blow the dragon flute, sound the crocodile drum!
Ah, singers with the dazzling teeth,
Slender dancing girls!
Now our time is running out, spring slipping past,
The peach blossom whirling down in a crimson rain,
I urge you to drink and be merry the whole day long,
For no wine will moisten the earth on a drunkard's tomb!

SIKONG TU

Sikong Tu (837-908), a native of Yongji County, Shanxi, was a celebrated poet and critic who passed the imperial examinations at the age of thirty-three and subsequently held several minor official posts. When the peasant insurgents led by Huang Chao stormed the Tang capital he fled, but later returned to rejoin the government. He retired to a life of seclusion at the age of 55. When the Tang Dynasty was overthrown, he refused a summon to serve the new regime and starved himself to death.

Brought up a Confucian, Sikong Tu later turned to Taoism and Buddhism and wrote poetry expressing his enjoyment of the natural world. His *The Twenty-four Modes of Poetry*, an analysis of poetic moods and styles, exercised a considerable influence on literary criticism in China.

The Twenty-Four Modes of Poetry

1. The Grand Mode

FULL play makes firm the outward flesh,
True substance gives inward fulness;
Returned to the Void, to the Absolute,
Grandeur comes of strength amassed;
Embracing all creation,
It spans infinitude,
Where surge the darkling clouds
And never-ceasing blow the rushing winds....
Transcend the outward form
To grasp what lies within;
Useless to strain for mastery,
Once yours it is a never-failing spring.

2. The Unemphatic Mode

IT dwells in quiet, in simplicity;
For inspiration is subtle, fugitive;
It drinks from the fountain of Great Harmony,
Flies with the solitary stork above;
Gentle as the breath of wind
That brushes your gown,
Or the rustling of tall bamboos
Whose beauty you long to convey;

Met by chance, it seems easy of access,
At your approach it withdraws
And, when you grope for it,
Slips through your hands and is gone!

3. The Ornate Mode

THE glint of rippling water,
Lush, distant green of spring,
And deep in the quiet valley
Glimpses of a lovely girl!
Peach trees are laden with blossoms
On wind-swept banks in the sun,
And the path winds, shaded by willows,
Where in flocks the orioles sing.
The further you press on,
The clearer your vision;
Infinite surely is the scene,
For ever changing and for ever new!

4. The Grave Mode

GREEN woods, a rustic hut,
And at sunset the air is clear,
As I stroll alone, bare-headed,
Hearing the fitful chirping of the birds.
No wild swan comes
With word from friend far away,
Yet in thought we are as close

As in days gone by.
Wind from the sea, an azure sky,
The moon is bright above the bank at night,
And I seem to hear your welcome voice,
Though the great river lies ahead.

5. The Lofty Mode

IMMORTALS borne upon pure air,
Lotus blooms in their hands,
Win through annihilation
To soar to trackless space;
Over the eastern Dipper rises the moon,
Sped by a beneficent wind;
Above Mount Hua the night is blue,
And men hear the clear toll of a bell...
Stand then apart in purity of heart,
Break through the confines of mortality,
Aloof as the Yellow Emperor and Yao,
Alone at the source of the Great Mystery.

6. The Polished Mode

A jade wine-pot brimming with spring,
A thatched hut to enjoy the rain,
And there sits a worthy scholar
With tall bamboos upon his left and right.
White clouds are scattering after rain,
Birds race past in the deep stillness;

Then pillowed on his lute in the green shade,
A waterfall cascading overhead,
As petals fall without a sound,
The man, serene as the chrysanthemum,
Sets down the season's glories —
Here is something well worth reading!

7. The Refined Mode

AS if mining gold
Or extracting silver from lead,
Give your whole heart to refining,
Make skimming off the dross a labour of love.
As spring water pours into deep pools,
And ancient mirrors give a true reflection,
One who is spotless and immaculate
May fly back on a moonbeam to the Truth.
Then raise your eyes to the stars
And sing of the hermit,
Today pure as flowing water,
His past life bright as the moon!

8. The Vigorous Mode

THE spirit wings as if through empty space,
And like a rainbow soars the vital force,
Rushing down sheer mountain gorges,
Swift as clouds before the wind!
Drink deep of Truth and feed on strength;

Store up simplicity within;
So will you be vigorous as the universe,
For this is to conserve your potency.
Be coeval with heaven and earth,
A co-worker in their miraculous mutations,
Make Actuality your goal,
And take as your guide the Finite.

9. The Exquisite Mode

INNATE nobility of mind
Sets little store by gold;
Colours laid on too thick must pall,
But light shades gain in depth.
Mist clearing by the stream,
Apricot blossom crimson in the glade,
A stately house beneath the moon,
A painted bridge in green shade,
A golden goblet brimming with wine,
A lute played for a friend...
Take these and be content,
For here is beauty enough to gladden the heart!

10. The Spontaneous Mode

STOOP and it is yours for the taking,
No boon to ask of neighbours;
Just follow the Way
And one touch of your hand brings spring,

Simple as finding a flower in bloom
Or watching the new year in!
No true gain can be snatched away,
What is seized is easily lost.
Like a recluse in the lonely hills
Gathering duckweed after rain,
May you become aware
Of the infinitude of all creation!

11. The Pregnant Mode

NOT a word said outright,
Yet the whole beauty revealed;
No mention of self,
Yet passion too deep to be borne;
And a true arbiter has the heart
To guide us as we drift,
Like wine bubbling over the strainer,
Abrupt return to autumn in blossom-time,
Dust whirled through space
Or foam flung up by the sea...
So the motley pageant converges only to scatter,
Till a myriad shapes are resolved at last in one.

12. The Uutrammelled Mode

FREE to study Nature's mysteries,
He breathes the empyrean;
His spirit grounded in Truth,

Sure of himself, he casts off all restraint.

Wide sweep the winds of heaven,

Grey loom the hills out at sea,

And with true strength imbued,

All creation spread before him;

He beckons sun, moon and stars,

Leads on the phoenix,

Drives the six tortoises[*] at dawn,

And washes his feet in the stream where rises the sun.

13. The Evocative Mode

THAT they might come back unceasingly,

That they might be ever with us!

The limpid pool clear to its depth,

The rare flower just opening,

The cockatoo of verdant spring,

The pavilion in the willows' shade,

The stranger from the blue hills,

The cup brimming with clear wine...

The living spirit travels far,

Untainted by dead ashes;

Such miracles of Nature,

Who is there to compass them?

---

* According to legend, these tortoises supported the earth.

14. The Well-Knit Mode

THE trail runs true
Yet seems beyond our ken;
And before the image takes shape
Strange changes come to pass.
Water flows, flowers blow,
The sun has not yet dried the limpid dew,
While travellers with far to go,
Tread with light steps and slow...
Writing rid of redundancy,
Thoughts free from stagnancy,
Are like the spring that makes all green
And clear as moonlight on the snow.

15. The Artless Mode

ABIDE by your nature
To grasp Truth untrammelled,
Rich with what comes to hand,
Following your bent.
Build a hut below the pines,
Read poems bare-headed,
Knowing only dawn and dusk,
Forgetful of time...
Then, if happiness is yours,
Why must there be action?
In this utter abandonment
Attain your end.

16. The Distinctive Mode

CLUMPS of slender pines
At whose feet clear water flows,
Bamboos muffled in dazzling snow,
Fishing-boats in the reach beyond;
And a scholar peerless as jade,
Strolling in search of seclusion,
Stays his steps to gaze
At the empty infinity of blue above...
Then strangely soars the spirit as of old,
Too ethereal to recall,
Like moonlight at dawn
Or autumn in the air.

17. The Devious Mode

GREEN and twisting the track
That leads up Mount Taihang;
Misty the veins deep in jade,
Faint the fragrance of flowers.
Like year-long toil in the fields,
Or strains of a Hunnish pipe,
It starts up again when you think it done,
Seems hidden but is then no more concealed.
Like the eddying ripples in water,
The circling flight of the roc,
The Way has no set pattern,
But fits both square and round.

18. The Natural Mode

CHOOSE plain words
To voice simple thoughts,
As if, meeting suddenly with a recluse,
You have a revelation of the Truth.
Beside the winding brook,
In the green shade of pines,
One man is gathering firewood,
Another playing the lute. . .
Follow your natural bent
And wonders come unsought;
So at a chance encounter
You hear rare music!

19. The Poignant Mode

A gale whips up the stream,
Trees in the forest crash,
And one in deathly anguish
Has called in vain for aid.
A hundred years slip by like water flowing,
Rank and riches are now cold ashes;
The Truth is ebbing away from day to day,
What hero, what talent, have we?
The fighter fondles his sword,
His heart flooded with grief,
As dead leaves patter to the ground
And rain drips on grey moss.

20. The Vivid Mode

ONLY the pure of heart
May recapture the Truth,
For this is seeking shadows on water
Or painting the glory of spring.
The changing shapes of wind-swept clouds,
The vividness of herb and flower,
The roaring waves of the ocean,
The rugged crags of mountains,
All these make up the great Truth
In one subtle medley of dust.
He who abandons the form to catch the likeness
Is true master of his craft!

21. The Transcendent Mode

FINER than the essence of the spirit,
More subtle than the secret springs of motion,
It is like floating on white clouds
Borne off by a fresh wind.
Afar, it seems at hand:
Approach, and it is gone;
Yet this inkling of Truth
Turns men from vulgar ways,
Like tall trees on rugged mountains,
Spring sunlight on green moss...
Dwell on it, ponder it;
Its faint music eludes the ear.

22. The Ethereal Mode

ALOOF from the world of men,
Apart from the vulgar crowd,
Like the stork on Mount Hou,
The cloud at the peak of Mount Hua,
A man of worth, his heart at peace,
Radiant with vital force,
Can ride the wind on a reed
And sail over the infinite.
Seemingly intangible,
Its echo is heard;
It is there for those who understand
But escapes those who would seize it

23. The Light-Hearted Mode

A man may live a hundred years,
And yet how short a span,
When joys are all so brief
And griefs crowd thick and fast!
Far better fill your cup with wine
And stroll each day among the misty vines
That flower above thatched eaves,
Or call on friends through the fine, drizzling rain;
Then, when the wine is drained,
Take up your cane and stroll off with a song.
Death comes at last to one and all:
Above us looms the southern hill!

24. The Flowing Mode

WHIRLING like water-wheels,
Rolling like beads;
Who can express
The animation of insensate form?
Immense, the axis of the earth,
Ever-turning, the pivot of heaven;
Let us grasp their clue
And blend with them into one,
Transcending the mind,
Returning again to the Void:
An orbit of a thousand years,
This is the key to my theme!

WANG YUCHENG

Wang Yucheng (945-1001), from a poor peasant family in Juye, Shandong, rose to become a court official after passing the imperial examinations. Upright and outspoken, he was demoted three times during his career.

The Bamboo Pavilion at Huanggang

THE district of Huanggang abounds in bamboos, the largest as big as rafters. Bamboo workers split the stems and slice off the knots, and the bamboo is used in place of earthen tiles. All the buildings here are roofed with these bamboo tiles because they are cheap and save labour. At the northwest corner of my city the walls had crumbled, the ground was overgrown with brambles, the place wild and dirty; so I had a small two-roomed pavilion constructed there, linking it with the Moon Wave Pavilion. It affords a view of the distant hills and dips at the shallows of the river below. The quiet seclusion there defies description. This pavilion is delightful during a sudden summer shower, when rain beats on the roof like a waterfall; it is equally delightful during heavy snow in winter, when the snow tinkles on the roof like jade. The pavilion is a good place for strumming a lyre, for the echo is smooth and mellow; it is a good place for chanting poetry too, for the recitation rings out fine and clear; it is a good place for playing draughts and hearing the sound made by draughtsmen on the board, or for playing cottabus and hearing the thud of arrows dropping into the pot; for all these sounds are brought out to the best advantage in this Bamboo Pavilion. In leisure moments after my official duties I put on a priestly gown and cap, take up the *Book of Change* and sit there in silence with incense burning to banish mundane cares. So, beside the river and hills, I watch the sails in the wind, the birds on the sand, the mist and clouds, the bamboos and the trees, and when I recover from the effects of wine, when my tea stops bubbling on the stove, I bid goodbye to the setting sun and welcome the rising of the white moon. Such are my pleasures in exile. Pavilions famed in history like the Cloud Reaching Pavilion, the Fallen Star Pavilion, the Well Frame Pavilion and the Splendid Pavilion, may have been superbly imposing and magnificent; but they served solely to entertain sing-song girls and dancers, a pastime hardly suited to a man of letters, and this is not my way. The bamboo workers tell me that bamboo tiles can last a bare ten years; while even if another layer is added, they last only twenty years. But I was sent to Chuzhou from the Imperial Academy in the first year of the Zhidao period (the year 995); the following year I was transferred to Guangling, and the year after that posted back to the Chancellor's Office. The next year, on New Year's Eve, I was ordered to proceed to Huangzhou, and I arrived in this prefecture in the third intercalary month of the following year. So the last four years have seen me incessantly on the move, and I have no idea where I shall be next year. Why, then, should I worry because this Bamboo Pavilion may not last? My one hope is that those who come here after me will continue to keep it up, so that this pavilion may go on standing for ever.

FAN ZHONGYAN

Fan Zhongyan (989-1015), a native of Wuxian County in Jiang-su, was not only a celebrated author but also a well-known states-man who held a number of important posts at court. His progres-sive ideals and advocacy of political reforms provoked opposition from conservative officials and he was forced to leave the capital and assume a local post in the northwest.

Much of Fan Zhongyan's poetry and prose, which is written in a lucid and lively style, has a distinctive political flavour.

Yueyang Pavilion

IN the spring of the fourth year of the Qingli period (the year 1044), Teng Zijing was banished from the capital to be governor of Baling Prefecture. After he had governed the district for a year, the administration became efficient, the people became u-nited, and all things that had fallen into disrepair were given a new lease of life. Then he restored Yueyang Pavilion, adding new splendour to the original structure and having inscribed on it poems by famous men of the Tang Dynasty as well as the present time. And he asked me to write an essay to commemorate this. Now I have found that the finest sights of Baling are concentrat-ed in the region of Lake Dongting. Dongting, nibbling at the dis-tant hills and gulping down the Yangtse River, strikes all behold-ers as vast and infinite, presenting a scene of boundless variety; and this is the superb view from Yueyang Pavilion. All this has been described in full by writers of earlier ages. However, since the lake is linked with Wu Gorge in the north and extends to the rivers Xiao and Xiang in the south, many exiles and wandering poets gather here, and their reactions to these sights vary great-ly. During a period of incessant rain, when a spell of bad weath-er continues for more than a month, when louring winds bellow angrily, tumultuous waves hurl themselves against the sky, sun and stars hide their light, hills and mountains disappear, merch-ants have to halt in their travels, masts collapse and oars splin-ter, the day darkens and the roars of tigers and howls of mon-keys are heard, if men come to this pavilion with a longing for home in their hearts or nursing a feeling of bitterness because of taunts and slander, they may find the sight depressing and fall prey to agitation or despair. But during mild and bright spring weather, when the waves are unruffled and the azure translucence above and below stretches before your eyes for myriads of *li*, when the water-birds fly down to congregate on the sands and fish with scales like glimmering silk disport themselves in the water, when the iris and orchids on the banks grow luxuriant and green; or when dusk falls over this vast expanse and bright moonlight casts its light a thousand *li*, when the rolling waves glitter like gold and silent shadows in the water glimmer like jade, and the fishermen sing to each other for sheer joy, then men coming up to this pavilion may feel complete freedom of heart and ease of spirit, forgetting every worldly gain or setback to hold their winecups in the breeze in absolute elation, delighted with life. But again when I consider the men of old who possessed true humanity, they seem to have responded quite differently. The reason, perhaps, may be this: natural beauty was not enough to make them happy, nor their own situation enough to make them sad. When such men are high in the government or at court, their first concern is for the people; when they retire to distant streams and lakes, their first concern is for their sovereign. Thus they worry both when in office and when in retirement. When, then, can they enjoy themselves in life? No doubt they are concerned before anyone else and enjoy themselves only after everyone else finds enjoyment. Surely these are the men in whose footsteps I should follow!

OUYANG XIU

Ouyang Xiu（1007-1072）, the son of a poor family from
Yongfeng in Jiangxi, is considered to embody the Song ideal of
the "renaissance" man. A distinguished historian, antiquarian
and bibliographer, he was also one of the outstanding statesmen
of his day. He was one of the leaders of the "ancient prose"
movement in literature, which advocated a return to ancient tradition as part of a programme of moral reform and regeneration.

The Roadside Hut of the Old Drunkard

THE district of Chu is enclosed all around by hills, of which those in the southwest boast the most lovely forests and dales. In the distance, densely wooded and possessed of a rugged beauty, is Mount Langya. When you penetrate a mile or two into this mountain you begin to hear the gurgling of a stream, and presently the stream — the Brewer's Spring — comes into sight cascading between two peaks. Rounding a bend you see a hut with a spreading roof hard by the stream, and this is the Roadside Hut of the Old Drunkard. This hut was built by the monk Zhi Xian. It was given its name by the governor, referring to himself. The governor, coming here with his friends, often gets tipsy after a little drinking; and since he is the most advanced in years, he calls himself the Old Drunkard. He delights less in drinking than in the hills and streams, taking pleasure in them and expressing the feeling in his heart through drinking. Now at dawn and dusk in this mountain come the changes between light and darkness: when the sun emerges, the misty woods become clear; when the clouds hang low, the grottoes are wrapped in gloom. Then in the course of the four seasons you find wild flowers burgeoning and blooming with a secret fragrance, the stately trees put on their mantle of leaves and give a goodly shade, until wind and frost touch all with austerity, the water sinks low and the rocks at the bottom of the stream emerge. A man going there in the morning and returning in the evening during the changing pageant of the seasons, can derive endless pleasure from the place. And the local people may be seen making their way there and back in an endless stream, the old and infirm as well as infants in arms, men carrying burdens who sing as they go, passers-by stopping to rest beneath the trees, those in front calling out and those behind answering. There the governor gives a feast with a variety of dishes before him, mostly wild vegetables and other mountain produce. The fish are freshly caught from the stream, and since the stream is deep the fish are fat; the wine is brewed with spring water, and since the spring is sweet the wine is superb. There they feast and drink merrily with no accompaniment of strings or flutes; when someone wins a game of cottabus or chess, when they mark up their scores in drinking games together, or raise a cheerful din sitting or standing, it can be seen that the guests are enjoying themselves. The elderly man with white hair in the middle, who sits utterly relaxed and at his ease, is the governor, already half drunk. Then the sun sinks towards the hills, men's shadows begin to flit about and scatter; and now the governor leaves, followed by his guests. In the shades of the woods birds chirp above and below, showing that the men have gone and the birds are at peace. But although the birds enjoy the hills and forests, they cannot understand men's pleasure in them; and although men enjoy accompanying the governor there, they cannot understand his pleasure either. The governor is able to share his enjoyment with others when he is in his cups, and sober again can write an essay about it. Who is this governor? Ouyang Xiu of Luling.

WANG ANSHI

Wang Anshi (1021-1086), an outstanding statesman, essayist and poet, was born into a lower middle-class family with a tradition of government service. He passed the imperial examinations in 1043 and then served in a number of different official posts. He introduced a sweeping programme of reforms known as the "New Policies", which were intended to revitalize the economy and reorganize and improve the civil service and the military. These met with widespread opposition from conservative elements in the government and Wang was forced to resign.

Wang Anshi wrote many poems which illustrate his great insight into social problems. He frequently wrote on historical subjects, using ancient themes as a pretext for expressing his own views on current affairs. His most popular poems, however, are those containing superb descriptions of nature and imparting his own keen enjoyment of life, all distinguished by their originality and aptness of imagery.

Confiscating Salt

GOVERNMENT orders rain down thick and fast,
Strict measures are taken at sea to confiscate salt,
And the poor wretches in their hovels sigh
As boats with officers and troops return.
Those islands have been barren from of old,
The rough islanders hard put to it to survive;
Unless they get salt from the sea they must surely starve,
But who would sit idle and submit to ruin?
So it is that pirates infest the seas,
Killing and robbing merchants and sinking their ships.
The people's livelihood is paramount,
Should those in power contend for such small pickings?

Thoughts

BEFORE ever I took up office
I grieved for the common people;
If a year of plenty cannot fill their bellies
What must become of them in flood or drought?
Though no brigands molest them,
How long can they last out?
Above all they dread the officials
Who ruin eight or nine households out of ten,

For when the millet and wheat fail in the fields
Without money for a bribe they cannot appeal for relief,
And those trudging to town to plead with the magistrate
Are whipped away from his gate.
Worst of all is the season when winter turns to spring,
Killing off the old and frail,
For the district head locks up the granaries
And county officials, cracking whips, levy taxes.
The villagers are squeezed dry,
The southern fields stripped of men,
Yet only a mite of the spoils goes to the state
While treacherous scoundrels prosper.
An official blind to this may rest content
And style himself "Father and Mother of the People";
But since I came to help govern this poor district
My heart fails me, shame overwhelms me,
For today I am the one responsible
For all that once appalled me.
Even a sage was hard put to it to manage government
    fields, *
And my abilities are of the meanest;
Self-reproach spurs me on to do my best,
And I share my worries with my colleagues.

_____

* Reference to a post once held by Confucius.

The Spring Wind

ALONE I ride north through the spring wind towards Yan
Past hills and streams strangely familiar:
Sunlight floats beyond the trees on the mighty river,
Dust rises above the plain like smoke from a fire;
Soft gold are the burgeoning willows in the sun,
The fresh green of the fields has been quickened by the rain;
And looking round in vain for magnolia trees
It dawns on me: A year has passed since I saw them bloom.

Written from Jinshan to Friends and Relatives

THE gateway to the sea spans Beigu's skyline,
The sandbanks in the mist recall Xixing;
The boats are gone but fluting can still be heard,
So remote the pavilions, only their lights are seen.

The moon on the hills is scattering gold through the pines,
The wind on the river whirls foam like crumbling snow;
I long to find a barge and float far east
To Fusang where the sun rises, but it cannot be!

Plum Blossom

SPRIGS of plum by the corner of the wall
Are blooming alone in the cold;
If not for the subtle fragrance drifting over
Who could tell this from snow on the boughs?

Going to the Countryside

THE whole plain is a tapestry of green
With no flower to be seen in the deep, shady woods;
Finding no blooms to caress, the wind and sun
Pay court instead to hemp and mulberry.

Written on the Wall for Master Huyin

HIS well-swept path under thatched eaves is clear of moss,
The flowers and trees here are planted by his hand;
A stream like an emerald girdle guards his fields
And the two hills confronting his gate cast a green shade.

Our Boat Moors at Guazhou

PARTED by a single stream, Jingkou and Guazhou;
Beyond a few hills, Mount Zhongshan;
Green in the spring wind the south bank of the Yangtse;
When will the bright moon light my journey home?

On the River

HALF lifted, the autumn mist north of the river,
But evening clouds heavy with rain are hanging low;
There seems no way through the green folds of hills,
Then a thousand sails, faint and clear, flash into sight.

Su Shi

Su Shi (1037-1101), also known as Su Dongpo, was born into a
family with a long tradition of government service in Meishan
County, Sichuan. The leading poet of the Northern Song period,
he was also a celebrated calligrapher and painter. He was a distinguished statesman and held many official posts, but was frequently banished.

Su often took a conservative political stand, opposing, for in-
stance, the reformist policies of Wang Anshi, but he played a
more progressive role in the world of letters by opposing the for-
malism then dominant. As well as *shi*, the classical verse form,
he also wrote *ci* poetry to melodies dating from the eighth century. He broadened the scope of *ci* poetry by introducing more serious subject matter and thus made it a more substantial genre.
His poetry is fresh and original and his prose is distinguished by
its vividness, rich imagery and boldness of vision.

Mountains Seen from the River

SEEN from our boat the mountains race like horses,
Hundreds of herds flash past;
The crags in front have changed shape suddenly,
The ridges behind tumble over each other in flight.
I look up at a small winding path
And the traveller high above, half lost to sight;
But even as I raise my hand to hail him
Our lone sail has scudded south like a bird on the wing.

To My Brother

Written in the saddle on the nineteenth of the eleventh month of the year Xinchou, * *after seeing Ziyou off outside the West Gate of Zhengzhou*

WHY, without wine, this drunken, dizzy feeling?
My heart is following the horseman home;
Your thoughts turn homeward now,
But what have I to cure my loneliness?
I climb a height for one last look at you —
Your black cap bobbing down the sunken road.
It is biting cold and you are thinly clad,

---

* 1061. Having seen the poet on his way to Fengxiang, where he was to be assistant magistrate, his brother started back to the capital. Ziyou had relinquished his own official post to be with their father.

Riding your lean nag alone through the fading moonlight.
Passers-by are singing, the stay-at-homes are merry;
My servants wonder why I look so sad.
I know life must have its partings,
But dread to think how quickly the years may pass.
I sit by my lamp in the cold, re-living the old days:
Remember, brother, our promise to listen together
To the patter of the rain at night again,
And never set your heart on official honours!

Recalling the Old Days at Mianchi

In the same rhymes as Ziyou's poem

TO what can we liken human life?
Perhaps to a wild swan's footprints on mud or snow;
By chance its claws imprint the mud
Before it flies off at random, east or west.
The old monk is dead and a new pagoda built; *
The old wall has crumbled, the poem we wrote on it
  gone. **
Do you still remember this rugged mountain path,
The long way, our exhaustion and how the lame donkey
  brayed?

---

* Monks were generally cremated and a pagoda built over their ashes.
** The poet and his brother had stayed in the temple here during a previous journey
  and written a poem on a wall.

A Visit to Jinshan Monastery*

THE Yangtse has its source in my home district,**
Serving the state I have followed its waves to the sea;
Tides here, they say, may rise a full ten feet;
On this cold day the sand still shows the traces;
This massive boulder south of Zhongling Fountain
Has been engulfed from of old to emerge again;
I climb to its top, gaze back towards my old home,
Yet see only green ranges north and south of the river.
Longing for home, I look for my boat to return,
But the monk makes me stay for sunset:
Countless ripples in the breeze seem creases in leather,
The ragged clouds in the sky are like red fish-tails;
The moon is a fragile crescent above the waves;
By the second watch it sinks, the sky turns black,
Then it seems as if a torch flares up in midstream,
Its flames lighting up the hills, startling the crows...
I go sadly to bed, not knowing
What this can be, the work of ghost or man?
Glorious river and hills — I should have retired!
The River God is shocked by my tardiness.
I apologize to the god: Don't get me wrong.
I vow by your river to return to my farm!

---

* In present-day Zhenjiang. The poet visited this famous old temple in 1071.
** The Su family came from Meishan in Sichuan.

Lake View Pavilion

Written when drunk on the twenty-seventh of the sixth month

CLOUDS black as spilt ink all but blotting out the hills,
Raindrops sprinkled like pearls leaping wildly into the boat;
A sudden wind sweeps the ground and scatters the storm,
Under Lake View Pavilion the water is clear as the sky.

Tame fish and turtles come swimming after men,
Here and there wild lotus bloom;
Pillowed on the waves we see hills rise and fall,
While in the breeze our boat drifts with the moon.

The Sight from Sea-View Pavilion at Dusk

THROUGH the pavilion blows the slanting rain,
Some poet should sing the splendour of this scene:
After rain the tide is still, blue the river and sea
Where lightning flickers like serpents purple and gold.

Lament of a Peasant Woman

THIS year the rice harvest is late,
Soon blighting winds will blow;
But before the wind comes torrential rain,
The sickle is rusted, the rake thick with mould.
She weeps till her eyes are dry, still the rain pours down;
It hurts to see the yellow ears flat in the mud!
A whole month she stays in a straw hut by the fields;
Once it clears, she reaps the rice and carts it home;
Sweating, shoulders chafed red, she carries her grain to
    market —
All she gets is the price of chaff!
She sells her ox to pay the tax, pulls down her hut for fuel,
Too simple to worry about next year's hunger;
Now the court demands money instead of rice,
To buy over the northwest tribesmen ten thousand *li* off.
The more wise men at court, the harder the people's lot —
Harder than being bride to the River God. *

---

* During the Warring States period there were serious floods in the kingdom of
Wei. To appease the God of the Yellow River, the people gave him a "bride" every year by throwing a girl into the river.

The Pavilion of Green Hills in Fahui Temple

MOUNT Wu assumes one form at dawn,
Another form at dusk;
Endless variety it has,
Shifting to feast your eyes.
Here a recluse has built a red pavilion,
With nothing round it in the solitude
But mounds a thousand paces wide
As screens on east and west.
Spring comes but brings no home-coming for me;
Autumn is sad, men say; but spring is sadder.
On the lake I recall the Brocade-Washing Stream; *
And these green hills remind me of Emei.
How long will these painted railings last?
He is growing old, the man leaning over the railings.
Success for a space, then decline — the pity of it!
Soon weeds and brambles will cover the pavilion,
And travellers in search of my old haunts
Will simply find Mount Wu spread out before them.

---

* The river at Chengdu.

On the Road to Xincheng

THE east wind knows of my journey home
And puts a stop to the drumming rain on my eaves;
Fair-weather clouds crown the hills like fleecy caps;
The morning sun hangs, a brass bell, over the trees;
The wild peach smiles by the low bamboo fence,
And the stream ripples clear over sand.
Happy the villagers in the western hills
Boiling bamboo shoots and celery for their ploughmen!

A Cloud-Burst at Youmei Hall*

A clap of thunder under the visitors' feet,
Massed clouds around too dense to sweep away;
A hurricane on the skyline whips up the sea,
And rain pelts down across the River Zhe
With the sparkle of wine brimming over a golden goblet,
The din of a thousand drumsticks on leather drums,
Heaven splashes the poet's face with water to wake him,**
And the mermaid's cave pours forth its treasures of jade and
    jasper.***

---

* Built on Mount Wu in 1057, it was the subject of poems by many writers.
** An allusion to an occasion when Emperor Xuanzong of the Tang Dynasty had Li
    Bai sprinkled with cold water to sober him up.
*** A legendary cave in the South Seas. The treasures here symbolize fine writing.

Abbot Zhan's Cell [*]

HE sounds the evening drum himself, the early morning
  bell;
His door closes on a single pillow, a flickering lamp;
After poking the red embers among white ashes
He lies down to hear the patter of rain on his window.

I Leave Town to See a Friend Off and, Missing Him, Stroll by the Stream

THE friend I came to see off has already gone,
The flowers I hoped to find have not yet bloomed;
But rather than return to town
I stroll beside the stream,
Till an old man greets me
And asks where I have been.
After good rain and snow this year,
They look forward to a thousand stacks of wheat.

---

[*] This abbot was in charge of the Monastery of Double Bamboos at Hangzhou.

Farewell to the Spring

Echoing Ziyou's poem

IN dream we may recapture spring,
But can these lines delay the sun's last rays?
Ill and far from home, after wine I long to sleep —
Even the honey-drunk bees are too lazy to fly.
Now peonies and cherry-blossom have fallen;
White-haired, on my monk's pallet, all cares forgotten,
Let me borrow your tome of Buddhist Law
To purge myself of vain and worldly thoughts.

A Poem

*Heavy snow on New Year's Eve kept me at Weizhou. New Year's
Day dawned clear and I resumed my journey, only to run into snow a-
gain.*

SNOW detained me on New Year's Eve,
Clear skies speed me on my way on New Year's Day;
The east wind scatters the fumes of last night's wine
As I jog along on my lean nag, half dreaming still
In the brilliant morning sunlight,
While a few last snowflakes whirl.
I dismount to drink in the open,
Lacking nothing now but someone to share my wine;

But at dusk clouds gather fast,

The whole air is thick with snow,

Flakes cling like goose feathers to my horse's mane,

And I marvel to find myself riding a white phoenix.

Three years of drought in the east

Emptied cottage after cottage, whole households fled;

Old peasants cast aside their ploughs and sighed,

Swallowing tears which stung their famished guts.

The snow is late this spring,

But it is not too late to sow spring wheat;

Why complain, then, of the hardships of the journey?

Rather let me sing of your good harvest to come.

The Moon at the Mid-Autumn Festival*

STILL the same friendly moon of last year,

Brimming over with radiance east of the old city;

While I, a wreck of the man I was last year,

Lie ill behind rickety windows.

Lingering, the moon contrives to seek me out;

Slender, she slips into my chamber;

How should she know of my illness?

She sees only that the Music Pavilion is empty.

---

* Written in 1078 in Xuzhou for his brother Ziyou, from whom he had parted the previous year in Nanjing.

I heave a deep sigh on my pillow,
Then leaning on a stick limp out behind her;
But the winds of heaven have no pity,
They blow me down from the jade palaces;
The chill dew penetrates my vital parts
Until I chirrup at night like a cricket in autumn;
I, once gallant as old Li Bai,
Reduced now to the dirges of Meng Jiao! *
How many years are left to me?
How many brilliant moons?
The cold fish, too, are sleepless,
All night they blow bubbles at each other.

Six years has this moon appeared,
Shining for five years on our separation;
Those songs at your departure
Moved all who heard to tears;
Ah, then was Nanjing truly a brave sight,
It was not an occasion to be lightly forgotten:
The hundred-acre lake like molten silver,
The moon hanging like a mirror in the sky!
At the third watch the music ended,
Men's shadows scattered through the deep green trees,
And back to the North Hall I went
As cold light flickered on the dewy leaves;
I called for wine, drank with my wife,
Thinking how I would recount this to my son,

---

* Another Tang-dynasty poet.

Little knowing that, old and ailing,
I should have no wine, nothing but pears and chestnuts.
East of the old river I can see
The flowering buckwheat make a carpet of snow;
But when I try to cap your last year's song,
My heart is close to breaking.

Now Shu* is by the River Wen,
Sitting alone behind closed doors,
And Zheng** is travelling north
In a solitary boat that sails through the night;
While Tun,*** though near at hand,
Is as inaccessible as if in gaol;
And Chao**** has sent me a letter
Echoing the old refrain.
Far away the thoughts of all four,
Sharing this brightness over a thousand *li*.
The moon does not know what it is to grow old:
We cannot enjoy this fine festival together!
When I think back to all the friends at that feast,
They have scattered like floating duckweed.
Tradition has it that the moon tonight
Is bright or dim for ten thousand *li* around;
And if such be the will of Heaven,
Let us not treat this festival lightly.

---

* His friend Shu Huan who was taking the examination at Yunzhou.
** Another friend Zheng Tin who had gone to his post at the capital.
*** Another friend Tun Qi who was also at Xuzhou taking an examination.
**** Another friend Chao Gaoqing who had just written to him.

Next year we must think of each other,
Overcoming the barriers of time and space.

On Li Sixun's Painting "Islets in the Yangtse"

GREY hills, a misty river,
In the middle of the Yangtse these two islands
Whose trackless cliffs the birds and monkeys shun,
Where only tall trees brush against the sky.
Whence then comes this small craft, its oarsmen's song
Floating now high, now low, out in midstream?
Smooth the sand, soft the breeze, unseen the shore;
Crags and boat play at seesaw, on and on....
Peaks like the dusky tresses of a girl
Who combs her hair at dawn before her mirror!
Enough of these wild fancies, all you merchants,
For this Fair Maid has married the Young Man![*]

---

* A pun on the names of one of the islands and a cliff near by.

On the Painting "A Wedding in Zhuchen Village" in Chen Jichang's Collection

I was prefect once of this district;
When apricots were in blossom
I went to this village to urge the farmers on.
But who could bear to paint the place today?
At night officers knock at the doors to levy money.

A Poem

After the rain I stroll to the fishpond below Four-View Pavilion, returning by way of the East Hill in front of Qianming Monastery

THE duckweed, parted by rain, closes ranks again,
Frogs are croaking on every side;
The crab-apple blossom has vanished like a dream,
And the new plums are nearly ripe enough to taste.
At leisure I carry herbs slung from my cane
Past the swing, now deserted,
Where tireless peonies alone
Are the rearguard of the spring.

The high pavilion has fallen into ruins,
Fish are raised in the pond below;
Dusk drifts in from the hills

And the spring wind is scented by meadows;
A hush has fallen over the market bridge,
Dark grown the bamboos round the old monastery;
Storks have come from none knows where
And their shrill cries fill the air as the sun sets.

The Red Plum

CAREFREE and indolent it blossoms late
But fearful lest cold beauty find no favour
Rouges its cheeks like peach or apricot,
Yet still retains its chill, austere aloofness.

Too cold at heart to follow the ways of the spring,
Its petals translucent as jade seem flushed with wine;
But the old poet, knowing nothing of the plum's nature,
Looks still for green leaves and verdant boughs.

The Lyre

SOME say music lurks in the lyre;
Why then, closed in its case is it dumb?
Some say the sound comes from the fingers of the player;
Why then on yours do we hear none?

The South Hall

I sweep the floor, light incense and close the door to sleep,
My mat smooth as water, my curtains gauzy as mist;
When a new arrival wakes me I wonder where I am,
For outside the west window waves stretch to meet the sky.

Crab-Apple

IN the spring breeze a blaze of flaming brightness,
A fragrant mist as the moon rounds the covered walk;
Afraid the flowers may fall asleep at night,
I light tall candles to shine on that crimson glory.

Written on the Wall of Xilin Monastery

THIS side a range of hills and there a peak:
From different vantage points, a different mountain.
To me it is not given to know the true face of Lushan
Because I am upon it.

Monk Huichong's Painting "Dusk on the Spring River"

TWO or three sprays of peach behind bamboo;
When spring warms the river the ducks are the first to know
   it;
Mayweed covers the ground, the reeds begin to shoot;
This is the season when porpoises swim upstream.

Written on a Painting of Autumn Scenery by Li Shinan

THE tide nibbles at the bank as it ebbs and flows,
Some frosty roots thrust out from the sparse wood;
To what port is the solitary boat returning?
Back to the village of yellow leaves south of the river.

A Head-Wind at Cihu Gorge

BRACED by its stays, the mast-head creaks and groans,
Sound sleeps the boatman in the foaming spray,
Well knowing his bamboo hawser,
Weak as it seems, will stand the wind's full fury.

A Lament for Lichees

EVERY ten *li* a station swirling with dust,

Every five *li* a post to urge couriers on;

Men die like flies, their corpses line the road,

So that lichees and longans may be delivered to court. *

Carriages race over hills, boats sweep through the seas,

With new plucked fruit on fresh boughs, the leaves still
   dewy,

All to win a smile from the beauty in the palace,

Though it cost bloodshed and strife, and its effect remains
   for ever.

In Han times the fruit was first fetched from the south;

In Tang times it was levied as yearly tribute from Sichuan;

And even today men would tear Li Linfu** limb from limb,

But no one pours a libation to Tang Qiang.***

I beg Heaven to pity our people,

And bring forth no more rare fruits to ruin them;

All they ask is timely rain, propitious winds

And an ample harvest to save them from cold and hunger.

Who has not seen the tea-leaves fine as grain beside the
   Wuyi stream

---

* Lichees and longans are delicious fruits grown in south China. The Emperor
   Minghuang (A. D. 713-756), to please his favourite Lady Yang, used to have
   them sent fresh post-haste to his court at Chang'an in northwest China, causing a
   great loss of lives on the way.

** The Tang-dynasty prime minister responsible for levying the tribute of lichees.

*** A Han-dynasty official who urged the emperor to abolish this tribute.

Which Ding and Cai* sent to the court as tribute?
Now men seize on fresh varieties to win favour
This year tea from Fujian was sent to the government too,
Yet our sovereign needs none of these.
How vulgar it is, this emphasis on high living!
What a pity that Lord Qian of Luoyang,** that loyal subject,
Should send tribute of peonies too.

An Impromptu Verse

A white-haired man, failing but full of zest,
Rests his ailing limbs on the wicker couch in his small study.
Tell them your master enjoys his sleep in spring,
That the priest may toll his bell at the fifth watch softly.

The Tide Pavilion at Chengmai***

I would gladly end my days in this South Sea village,
But the Jade Emperor sends a witch to summon my spirit.
Far off at the low horizon the hawk disappears
And there — that faint line of green hills — is the Middle
   Kingdom.

---

  * Ding Jinggong and Cai Junmo were Song-dynasty officials.
 ** Qian Weiyan was another high official of the Song Dynasty.
*** In Hainan Island.

A Dream of My Wife*

*Recording my dream on the night of the twentieth of the first month of the year Yimao***

TEN years parted, one living, one dead;

　Not thinking

　Yet never forgetting;

A thousand *li* from her lonely grave

I have nowhere to tell my grief;

Yet should we meet again she would hardly know

　This ravaged face,

　These temples tinged with grey.

At night in a dream I am suddenly home again:

　By my small study window

　She sits at her dressing-table;

We look at each other and find no words,

But the tears course down our cheeks.

Year after year heart-broken I fancy her

　On moonlit nights

　By the hill covered with young pines.

---

* The following nine poems are written in the *ci* form.

** 1075. Ten years previously his wife had died and been buried at Meizhou. Su Shi planted thousands of pine seedlings round the graveyard.

Hunting at Mizhou*

OLD limbs regain the fire of youth:
Left hand leashing a hound,
On the right wrist a falcon.
Silk-capped and sable-coated,
A thousand horsemen sweep across the plain;
The whole city, it's said, has turned out
To watch His Excellency
Shoot the tiger!
Heart gladdened by wine,
Who cares
For a few white hairs?
But when will the court send an envoy
With an imperial tally to pardon the exile?
That day I will bend my bow like a full moon
And aiming northwest
Shoot down the Wolf** from the sky!

---

* The poet served as magistrate of Mizhou in 1075 and 1076. It was a poor district,
  where officials under a cloud were sent.
** Sirius, standing here for the Qiang tribesmen then fighting with the Hans.

The Moon Festival

On the Mid-Autumn Festival of the year Bingchen * *I drank happily till dawn and wrote this in my cups while thinking of Ziyou.*

BRIGHT moon, when was your birth?
Winecup in hand, I ask the deep blue sky;
Not knowing what year it is tonight
In those celestial palaces on high.
I long to fly back on the wind,
Yet dread those crystal towers, those courts of jade,
Freezing to death among those icy heights!
Instead I rise to dance with my pale shadow;
Better off, after all, in the world of men.

Rounding the red pavilion,
Stooping to look through gauze windows,
She shines on the sleepless.
The moon should know no sadness;
Why, then, is she always full when dear ones are parted?
For men the grief of parting, joy of reunion,
Just as the moon wanes and waxes, is bright or dim:
Always some flaw — and so it has been since of old.
My one wish for you, then, is long life
And a share in this loveliness far, far away!

---

* 1076.

Five Poems

*Made on my way to offer thanks for rain at the Rocky Pool outside
Xuzhou. This pool lies twenty li east of the city, rising or falling with
the River Si and turning clear or muddy like the river.*

A warm red in the sunlight the pool where fish can be seen,
And green the shade of the village trees where crows hide
    themselves at dusk;
Here gather small boys and greybeards with twinkling eyes;
The deer are startled at the sight of men,
But monkeys come unbidden at the sound of drums.
This I tell the girls picking mulberries on my way home.

A hasty prinking and in small groups girls gather
By their wicker gates to see the governor,
Squeezed close, they stepped on each other's madder-dyed
    skirts;
Old and young, all turn out to harvest the wheat;
Crows and kites wheel over the sacrifice in the village;
And old tipplers are sleeping it off in the road at dusk.

THICK, thick the jute leaves, lush the hemp;
One family boiling cocoons scents the whole village;
Across the fence the prattle of girls reeling silk,
Grandads with sticks are nodding tipsily;
New wheat is picked, flour ground to ease my hunger,
As I ask when the bean leaves will begin to yellow.

DATE-flowers fall rustling on my gown,

Spinning-wheels whirr at both ends of the village,

One in fibre cape sells cucumber under the willow...

Drowsy with wine, so far to go, I feel an urge to sleep;

The sun is high and, parched, longing for tea,

I knock at a cottage door to try my luck.

SOFT grass, fresh-washed by rain;

Light sand where horses raise no dust:

Shall I ever be free to plough the fields again?

In warm sunlight hemp and mulberry glint like water,

The breeze is spiced with mugwort and artemisia —

This, surely, is where I belong!

Caught in the Rain

On the seventh day of the third month we were caught in the rain on our way to Shahu. The umbrellas had gone ahead, my companions were quite downhearted, but I took no notice. It soon cleared, and I wrote this.

FORGET that patter of rain on the forest leaves,

Why not chant a poem as we plod slowly on?

Pleasanter than a saddle this bamboo staff and straw

    sandals —

        Here's nothing to fear!

I could spend my whole life in the mist and rain.

The keen spring wind has sobered me,
Left me chilly,
But slanting sunlight beckons from high on the hill;
One last look at the bleak scene behind
And on I go,
Impervious to wind, rain or sunny weather.

Memories of the Past at Red Cliff[*]

EAST flows the mighty river,
Sweeping away the heroes of time past;
This ancient rampart on its western shore
Is Zhou Yu's Red Cliff of Three Kingdoms' fame;
Here jagged boulders pound the clouds,
Huge waves tear banks apart,
And foam piles up a thousand drifts of snow;
A scene fair as a painting,
Countless the brave men here in time gone by!
I dream of Marshal Zhou Yu in his day
With his new bride, the Lord Qiao's younger daughter,
Dashing and debonair,
Silk-capped, with feather fan,
He laughed and jested
While the dread enemy fleet was burned to ashes!

---

[*] Scene of the battle in A.D. 208 when Liu Bei and Sun Quan defeated Cao Cao's advancing forces.

In fancy through those scenes of old I range,
My heart overflowing, surely a figure of fun,
    A man grey before his time.
    Ah, this life is a dream,
Let me drink to the moon on the river!

At Tinghui Abbey in Huangzhou

FROM a sparse plane-tree hangs the waning moon,
Now are clepsydras still, men's voices hushed;
Who is there to see the recluse pacing up and down,
A solitary swan on the blurred horizon?
Startled into flight he turns back,
But there is none to understand his grief;
He wings past the frozen boughs and will not roost,
Lonely on the chill sandbank in the river.

Willow Catkins

SO like a flower and yet no flower,
Her fall goes unlamented;
Spurning her home for the roadside,
She has her fancies, fickle yet not unfeeling,
Like tender thoughts entangled,
Or drowsy, lovely eyes

That fain would open.
In dream she drifts with the wind ten thousand *li*
To seek out her beloved,
Till she is wakened
By the oriole's cry.
Grieve not when all the catkins fall,
But sigh for red petals left to lie in the yard;
A shower of morning rain
And they are gone,
Scattered like weeds in the pool;
Of spring's colours now
Two-thirds lie in the dust,
One-third in the flowing stream.
Yet when you look close these are not willow catkins,
But, drop upon drop,
The tears of parted lovers.

Song

LAST red of blossoms fades,
Green are the apricots and small;
Now swallows skim
While emerald waters wind about the house,
And though most catkins have been blown away
No place on earth but the sweet grass will grow!
Within the wall a swing, without the highway;
There, passers-by,

And here sweet girlish laughter.
But all too soon it fades away, that laughter,
Heart-breaking for a man with too much heart!

First Visit to the Red Cliff

IN the autumn of the year Renxu (1082), at the time of the full
moon in the seventh month, I went by boat with some friends to
the Red Cliff. There was a fresh, gentle breeze, but the water
was unruffled. I raised my winecup to drink to my friends, and
we chanted the poem on the bright moon, singing the stanza
about the fair maid. Soon the moon rose above the eastern mountain, hovering between the Dipper and the Cowherd. The river
stretched white, sparkling as if with dew, its glimmering water
merging with the sky. We let our craft drift over the boundless
expanse of water, feeling as free as if we were riding the wind
bound for some unknown destination, as light as if we had left
the world of men and become winged immortals. Drinking, we
became very merry; and we sang a song, beating time on the side
of the boat. This was the song:

Our rudder and oars, redolent of cassia and orchids;
Strike the moon's reflection, cleaving the glimmering water;
But my heart is far away,
Longing for my dear one under a different sky.

One friend, who was a good flutist, played an accompaniment

to this song. The notes rang out nostalgic, mournful and plaintive, trailing on and on like a thread of gossamer, arousing the serpents lurking in dark caverns, drawing tears from a widow in her lonely boat. Sad at heart, I sat up straight to ask my friend why the music was so mournful.

He replied, "Didn't Cao Cao[*] describe a scene like this in his poem: 'The moon is bright, the stars are scattered, the crows fly south. . . .'? And isn't this the place where he was defeated by Zhou Yu? See how the mountains and streams intertwine, and how darkly imposing they are with Xiakou to the west and Wuchang to the east. When Cao Cao took Jingzhou by storm and conquered Jiangling, then advanced eastward along the river, his battleships stretched for a thousand *li*, his armies' pennons and banners filled the sky. When he offered a libation of wine on the river and lance in hand chanted his poem, he was the hero of his times. But where is he now? We are mere fishermen and woodcutters, keeping company with fish and prawns and befriending deer; we sail our skiff, frail as a leaf, and toast each other by drinking wine from a gourd; we are nothing but insects who live in this world but one day, mere specks of grain in the vastness of the ocean. I am grieved because our life is so transient, and envy the mighty river which flows on for ever. I long to clasp winged fairies and roam freely, or to embrace the bright moon for all eternity. But knowing that this cannot be attained at once, I give vent to my feelings in these notes which pass with the sad breeze."

---

* Famous general and statesman in the third century. He tried to conquer the Kingdom of Wu, but was defeated by the Wu general Zhou Yu in 208.

Then I asked him, "Have you considered the water and the moon? Water flows away but is never lost; the moon waxes and wanes, but neither increases nor diminishes. If you look at its changing aspect, the universe passes in the twinkling of an eye; but if you look at its changeless aspect, all creatures including ourselves are imperishable. What reason have you to envy other things? Besides, everything in this universe has its owner; and if it does not belong to me not a tiny speck can I take. The sole exceptions are the cool breeze on the river, the bright moon over the hills. These serve as music to our ears, as colour to our eyes; these we can take freely and enjoy for ever; these are inexhaustible treasures supplied by the Creator, and things in which we can delight together."

My friend was pleased and laughed. Then we rinsed our cups and filled them with wine again. When we had finished the dishes, and cups and plates lay about us in disorder, we stretched out in the boat and did not notice the coming of dawn in the east.

Second Visit to the Red Cliff

IN the tenth month of the same year when the moon was full, I set off on foot from Snow Hall to return to Lingao, accompanied by two friends. Our way lay past Yellow Mud Slope. There had been frost and dew, and the trees had lost all their leaves; our shadows were reflected on the ground and looking up we caught sight of the bright moon. Gazing round in delight, we sang a chorus as we walked along. Then I sighed and said, "Here we have friends but no wine; and even if we had wine, we have no dishes to go with it. The moon is bright and the breeze fresh — how shall we spend such a fine evening?"

One of my friends replied, "Just before dusk today I caught a fish in my net. It has a large mouth and small scales and is something like a perch from the River Song. But where can we get wine?"

When we reached home, I consulted my wife, and she said, "I have kept a flagon of wine for some time, storing it away in case you might need it suddenly." So taking the wine and fish, we went to pay another visit to the Red Cliff.

The river flowed noisily through riven cliffs that towered a thousand feet; the high hills dwarfed the moon, and the water had sunk so low that rocks emerged. Although it was not long since my previous visit, the scenery had changed out of recognition. Then I girded up my gown to climb, stepping on jagged crags, parting the thick-growing brambles, crouching on boulders shaped like tigers and leopards, ascending through creepers resembling dragons and serpents, till I reached the perilous eyrie of the hawk to look down on the dark abode of the water god. My two friends were unable to follow me, however. Then I started singing aloud. The trees and bushes trembled, the hills and dales re-echoed, a wind sprang up and waves surged. Struck by the quiet and awed by the solitude, I felt this was no place in which to linger. So I turned back and reached our boat. We let our craft drift in mid-stream, allowing it to float where it would. It was nearing midnight and all around was still. A lonely crane flew from the east across the river. It had wings like cartwheels, was clothed in black and white feathers. With a long, shrill cry it flew west passing our boat. Later, when my friends had left and I was in bed, I dreamed I saw a Taoist priest in flowing feathery garments pass my house at Lingao. He bowed and said, "Did you enjoy your visit to the Red Cliff?" When I asked his name, he bent his head and gave no answer. "Ah, I know!" I cried. "Aren't you the one who flew past me with a cry last night?" The priest glanced at me with a smile. Then I woke with a start. But when I opened the door to have a look, I could find no trace of him.

CHAO BUZHI

Chao Buzhi (1053-1110), a native of Juye in Shandong, passed the imperial examinations at the age of seventeen and subsequently held various minor official posts. He was banished because he advocated the recovery of lost territory and henceforth led the life of a recluse. He writes in a vivid and fluent style which clearly illustrates his debt to Su Shi.

A Visit to the Hills North of Xincheng

THIRTY *li* north of Xincheng we found ourselves deep in the hills, and the trees and plants, springs and rocks there had a more secluded look. At first we could still ride through the jagged boulders. On both sides of us were huge pine trees, some curving down like awnings, some looming up like obelisks, some standing erect like men, some reclining like dragons. Under the pines among the grass a low stream meandered unseen, to cascade at last down a stone vault with a tinkling sound. Between the pines were vines dozens of feet long, writhing like enormous serpents. Above was a black bird reminiscent of a mynah with a red crest and long beak, and this lowered its head to peck at the trees and screech. A little to the west rose a peak, high and sheer, with a tiny footpath up it just wide enough for one. We tethered our horses to the crags and climbed up helping each other to ascend. There was such an abundance of bamboos that looking up we could not see the sun. After proceeding for four or five *li*, we heard the cackling of fowls. A monk in a cloth gown came towards us, but when we addressed him he started and looked away, as difficult to approach as a wild stag. On the summit was a building of a few dozen rooms with balustrades which followed the curve of the cliff. We trailed round and round through these like snails or rats, before finally emerging, for the doors and windows were built facing each other. Then we sat down to rest. A gust of wind on the mountain, and all the bells in the halls and courts started jangling. We looked around in amazement, marvelling at the strange place to which we had come. Since dusk was falling, we stayed there. It was then the ninth month. The sky seemed lofty, the dew was glistening, the mountain appeared deserted and the moon was bright. When we looked up the stars, very large and brilliant, seemed to be hanging just above our heads. Outside the window grew a few dozen bamboos which rustled against each other with a ceaseless swishing sound, while some plums and palms stood out among the bamboos like goblins with bristling hair, so that gazing around we were disturbed in spirit and could not sleep. At dawn we left. We returned home a few days later still under the spell of this place, and I have written this to record the occasion. We never went back there, but often dream of those hills.

Lu You

Lu You (1125-1210), from Shaoxing in Zhejiang, was born when the Nüzhen Tartars had overrun much of North China. He held a succession of minor official posts but was unable to effect any of the political reforms he advocated. In 1172, he began to serve in the army on the Sichuan-Shaanxi border. It is known that sometime later he was dismissed from a post in Jiangxi for distributing government grain to relieve famine. Lu You was a prolific poet and more than nine thousand of his poems have survived. His work is noted for its ardent patriotism.

A Visit to a Village West of the Mountains

DON'T sneer at the lees in the peasants' wine,
In a good year they've chicken and pork to offer guests.
Where hills bend, streams wind and the pathway seems to
    end,
Past dark willows and flowers in bloom lies another village.
They greet the spring sacrifice here with pipes and drums,
And dress simply, keeping up the old traditions.
Some evening when I'm free and there is moonlight,
I shall stroll over with my stick and knock at their gate.

A Journey South of the Mountain

THREE days have I journeyed south of Zhongnan Mountain
On a highway running straight from east to west;
The plain, flat and fertile, stretches out of sight,
Green the wheat fields, dense and dark the mulberry trees.
Close to Hangu Pass and the old land of Qin
The mettlesome people swing and play ball together;
Thick grows the alfalfa, the horses here are sturdy;
Willows line the roads and carts go rumbling past. . .
Here kingdoms rose and fell in days gone by,
But the hills and streams are unchanged;

Chill clouds hang low over the Marshal's Altar,*
The spring sun sets before the Minister's Temple.**
Two score years and more we have lost the Central Plain,
Hard to win it back from the Yangtse and Huai valleys;
But let our troops descend with sounding drums
From their base on this high plateau within the Pass.

Encountering Light Rain at Sword Pass

MY clothes are soiled with dust and stained with wine,
But each stage of the long journey is entrancing...
And I ask myself: Am I a poet,
Jogging through Sword Pass on my donkey in light rain?

Written in My Cups at Night on the Seventeenth of the Third Month

I carved a whale that year in the Eastern Ocean,
Gave play to my valour among white waves mountain-high;
In the Southern Hills last autumn I shot a tiger,
And snow muffled my sables as home I rode by night...

---

* Where Han Xin was appointed commander of the Han forces in 206 B.C.
** The temple of Zhuge Liang, prime minister of the kingdom of Shu in the third century.

How ridiculously have I aged this year!
I wince at the grey hair, the wan face in my mirror;
And only when wine rekindles the old fires
Do I bare my head and shout defiance again.
While the Tartar hordes run wild, my heart cannot rest,
My sword clangs solitary by my bed;
The light gutters out as I wake in the shabby post-house,
Storm batters the windows and the third watch sounds.

The Review at Jiazhou on the Twenty-Second of the Eighth Month

BOWS and swords by the road surround the deputy, *
Banners by the stream billow in the autumn wind;
The scholar dons close-fitting uniform again,
And carved bugles add fresh might to this mountain province.
A censor when young whose proposals passed unheeded,
Then an adviser who accomplished nothing,
I know that vermin are easily wiped out
And long to harness the River of Heaven to scour the Central Plain. **

---

* Lu You was then deputy prefect of Jiazhou in western Sichuan.
** The River of Heaven was the Milky Way. The Central Plain was the Yellow River Valley then occupied by the Nüzhen Tartars.

News Comes of Fighting Among the Tartars

THAT year we campaigned south of the Southern Hills,

Often riding out to hunt at night after drinking;

The game piled up: black bears, grey rhinoceros...

And bare-handed I dragged back a shaggy tiger.

At times I climbed a height, gazed towards Chang'an,

And chanted my grief to the sky while my tears fell like rain.

Now my grey hair betrays my age,

Yet I long to lay down my life for my noble lord.

When word comes of wars among the Tartar tribes

I fondle my blade in the autumn wind, and tears

Will not let me speak of the Eight Tombs at Luoyang, *

Dust-stained sepulchres among the chilly pines...

I am nearing fifty and wear a scholar's cap

When I long to wear riding breeches;

An old charger brooding in his box, ashamed,

Not even a "dried fish ferried across the river"!**

---

* The tombs of the emperors of the Northern Song Dynasty.

** An allusion to the Han folk song, *A Dried Fish*:

　　The dried fish, ferried across the river, weeps;

　　Too late he repents his folly!

　　He writes a letter to the bream and tench

　　Warning them to be more wary!

Song of the Sword

THE good sword under the recluse's pillow
Clangs faintly all night long.
Men tell of swords changing to dragons
And this may forebode a storm;
For, angered by the frenzied Tartar hordes,
It longs to serve in distant expeditions,
I fetch wine and pour a libation to the sword:
A great treasure should remain obscure;
There are those who know your worth,
When the time comes they will use you.
You have ample scope in your scabbard,
Why voice your complaints?

A Stroll Through Some Gardens in Blossom Time

A passion for flowers has driven me distracted,
What if sun or wind should spoil their crimson sweetness?
I pen my plea at night to the Bright Hall of Heaven,
Craving dull days to preserve the apple blossom.

Rain

A glimmer in the air like threads of silk,
Then, of a sudden, barbed shafts strike the ground;
Dark still within the curtains, he dreams past dawn,
His spring coat drying over the bronze censer.
Plop, plop! Fish from the pool leap into the canal.
Whirr, whirr! The swallows skim back to their nests on the
    beams.
No wind can blow down the fallen blossom now
Which clings crimson and wet to the boughs.

Thoughts While Passing a Farm-House

WITH loose reins by the river I follow the setting sun.
Whose well and mortar are these by the wicker gate?
Behind the fence a dog barks at passers-by,
Silkworms hungry on their frame wait for mulberry leaves.
These ten years have disgusted me with the world and its
    ways,
My home ten thousand *li* away is blurred even in dreams.
Farming is a fit task for heroes,
And there are worse ends than to die of old age on a farm.

Archery Practice by the River at Wanli Bridge

RIDGES sweep like waves northeastwards,
From my chair on a fine spring day I watch the archers;
The warm breeze slowly saps the carved bow's strength,
But far off we hear the twang of feathered arrows.
We shall surely shoot down the comets from the sky, *
The foxes and hares in the grass need have no fear.
As long as I live who knows what may come to pass?
With one arrow I may yet recapture a hundred towns.

Moonlight Over the Mountain Pass

FOR fifteen years we have made peace with the Tartars,
Our frontier generals rest idle, their swords sheathed;
Deep within vermilion gates there is singing and dancing,
Horses die plump in their stables, bow-strings are broken,
And the tocsin simply hastens the waning moon,
While the hair of the men who joined up at thirty is white.
Who can gauge a soldier's heart from the sound of his flute?
Did they perish in vain, those whose bones gleam white on
    the sand?
Since ancient times war has raged on the Central Plain —
Will the sons of the Huns plague us still, and their sons'
    sons?

---

* i.e. the Tartar invaders in the north.

A subject people, weary to death, longs for freedom,
There is no counting the tears that flow tonight!

Song of the Northern Border

ONE sword thrust and the mountain splits apart,
One battle cry and the city wall tumbles down;
Past counting our host's armoured men and chargers
That surge forward, a silver mountain shaking the earth.
With long spears we hunt tigers north of the Qilian range, *
A bloody carcass is dragged before my horse;
Then off to shoot wild geese on the shore of the Yalu; **
Arrows fly and the geese take wing darkening the sky.
On the grassy bank of a clear stream we halt,
Pitch tents, kill oxen and drink deep of wine;
Not for us the ways of the young nobles at court
And the childish pranks they play with whisks and spittoons.

Going down the Yangtse from Yiling

DRUMS and bugles thunder, shaking the river bank,
Passing a hundred shoals the way seems to end,

---

* The Qilian Mountains are in Gansu in northwest China.
** The Yalu River is on the northeast frontier of China.

But the hills dip, the river flows on to the grey horizon
And earth and sky open out as we point ahead.
Swift kestrels sweep across the distant shore,
Great fish leap up as if to soar to heaven.
Do you know, friend, what gladdens my heart today?
That yellow flag, thirty feet high, fluttering in the wind.

Passing Mount Lingshi

PEAKS looming strange before my horse appal me;
The mountains of Wu and Shu are nothing to this,
So green, so dark, soaring sheer into space...
Too bad to confine this giant within one small verse!

A Snowstorm on the Way to Yiyang

DUSK fell on the river shore but I rode on
Till a great snow filled the air, blotting all from view;
A brave sight, white bucklers descending from the sky
Drawing up on earth in splendid battle array.
In my youth I loved life in the army,
Chafing at the restrictions of an official post;
How often I gazed from my saddle with wistful eyes,
Eager to sweep clear the Central Plain for my lord.

That night the hiss of snow on my papered windows

Fell on my ears like the clash of iron-clad horses.

I rose, poured wine and sang a marching song

To still the tumult of the host in my breast.

A Poem

Towards midnight on the eleventh of the fifth month, I dreamed that I accompanied the emperor's army to restore all the lost territory of Han and Tang. I saw a rich, populous city and was told that this was Liangzhou. In my joy I started to write a poem in the saddle, but woke before it was finished. Now I am completing it.

SINCE the time of Tianbao, when two capitals fell to the
    Huns,

No Han garrison has been stationed in the northwest,

For five centuries the land has been abandoned.

Now our sage ruler issues the order and heads the campaign,

A million warriors follow the Son of Heaven;

Before his command goes out our land is retaken,

Ramparts are built far away, new maps presented,

Guards drawn up by the emperor's tent, amnesties pro-
    claimed;

Hills and streams as far as eye can see are ours,

Documents in these regions use the Chunxi era;

Now six regiments of guards are fine in brocade,

Drums and bugles fill the air in the autumn wind,

The foot of Alfalfa Peak bristles with defences
And beacons are flaring all the way to Turfan,
While the girls of Liangzhou, crowding their high towers,
Are combing their hair like the women of the capital.

I Climb Yixian Tower in the Rain to Watch the River Rise

A rainy vapour veils a thousand peaks,
The river's thunder shakes ten thousand homes;
Clouds burst, the whole sky blackens,
Foam is tossed through the air like blossom,
Waves surge through empty pavilions,
Broken rafts bob up and down...
My thoughts turn to that stirring voyage in days gone by,
That intoxicating descent through the Yangtse Gorges!

A Poem

Written at night on the twenty-eighth of the seventh month in delight at rain after a bad spell of drought

GOOD crops have shrivelled, only the weeds are green,
One cannot sleep at night for worrying;

Then, sweeter than heavenly music,
Comes the sound of rain cascading off the eaves.

My Small Garden

HAZY grass links my small garden with my neighbours'
And mulberry trees cast shadows across the path.
I lie reading Tao Yuanming's poems, * but halfway through
A drizzle starts and I go to weed my melon patch.

Calligraphy

ALL my money has gone on three thousand gallons of wine,
Yet they cannot overcome my infinite sadness;
As I drink today my eyes flash fire,
I seize my brush and look round, the whole world shrinks,
And in a flash, unwitting, I start to write.
A storm rages in my breast, heaven lends me strength,
As when dragons war in the waste, murky, reeking of
  blood,
Or demons topple down crags and the moon turns dark,

---

* A fifth-century poet whose best poems, about country life, were written after his
retirement from office.

In this moment all sadness is driven from my heart,
I pound the couch with a cry and my cap falls off.
The fine paper of Suzhou and Chengdu will not serve,
Instead I write on the thirty-foot wall of my room.

Thoughts Before Dawn in Autumn as I Step Through the Wicker Gate for a Breath of Fresh Air

A thousand miles the river flows east to the sea.
A million feet the mountain soars to the sky;
But the tears of the conquered are lost in Tartar dust,
One more year must they watch the south for our emperor's
   arms!

The Great Storm on the Fourth of the Eleventh Month

STARK I lie in a lonely village, uncomplaining,
And dream of defending Karashar for our state;
Late at night on my couch I hear the driving rain,
Iron-clad steeds cross a frozen river in my dreams.

Fallen Plum Blossom

CRUEL snow and raging wind bring out its courage,
Staunchest and noblest of flowers!
Its day done, it is content to drift away,
And would think shame to beg the spring for mercy.

Half drunk, I pluck two sprays of faded plum,
Caring nothing if peach and cherry are all the fashion;
For when the ground is locked in ice and snow,
This is the flower that brings spring back again.

Lament for a Peasant Household

HE has sown every slope with wheat,
Sown every stream with paddy,
His oxen's necks are rubbed raw to the bone,
Yet still at night he goads them on to plough.
His last ounce of strength goes into farming,
And all he asks is to be left in peace;
But who is this come knocking at his door?
The county officer clamouring for taxes!
He is haled to the county court,
Bastinadoed day and night;
All men dread death,
But he sees no way out...

Home again he longs to tell his wrongs,
Yet shrinks from upsetting his parents,
For to provide the two old folk with food,
He is ready to sacrifice his wife and son.

Old and Ailing

OLD and ailing, of no use to this great age,
I may still pick chrysanthemums by the eastern fence;
So poor that when I hold up the skirt of my gown,
My elbows show through the holes in my ragged sleeves;
When I shrug my shoulders, my shoulder-blades stick out...
Half my days have been spent in drinking,
And nothing is left of my life's work but some poems;
But no matter if no one shares my views today,
I can wait for those yet to come!

Rain in Early Spring

THE paddy fields thirst for rain,
But the silkworm frames dread the cold;
Those who live behind vermilion gates are harder to under-
    stand —
They fear lest rain should spoil their peonies.

To My Son

DEATH ends all, that is sure,
But what grieves me is not to have seen our land united;
The day that our imperial arms win back the Central Plain,
Mind you sacrifice and let your old man know!

FAN CHENGDA

Fan Chengda (1126-1193) was born into a poor family in Wuxian in Jiangsu. He passed the highest of the imperial examinations at the age of twenty-eight and subsequently had a successful official career. Owing to illness, he resigned at the age of fifty-six and settled down at Shihu.

A major poet of the Southern Song (1127-1279), Fan Chengda's writing evidences his distress at the suffering of ordinary people and at the social iniquities of the period. The best of his nearly two thousand poems describe rural life and are written in an original style marked by its freshness and poignancy.

Reeling Silk

GREEN, green the wheat, golden the barley,
The sun comes up over the plain, the day is cool,
And sisters-in-law urge each other to make haste,
Their front yards sweet from cocoons boiled in the back.
Whirr, whirr! The spinning wheels turn fast as wind,
Plump the cocoons and unbroken the long threads;
But this year no clothes will be woven,
They must sell their silk tomorrow at the West Gate.

Two Songs of Kuizhou

1

IN the new town's orchard west of the mountain stream
Loquats weigh down the trees and the apricots are round;
Folk sell them half-green and half-yellow in the morning,
Coming home again with salt and wine at noon.

2

THE fields on the hill are a patchwork of green and red
Now the millet is in ear, the beans growing like bushes;
How soft it is, the rice from the eastern plain,
But none finds its way into the rice bins of the poor.

Thoughts on Hearing the Wretched Cries of a Fishmonger Outside the Wall in the Snow

DRIVEN out by his rice bowl, what man dare rest idle?
Snow comes up to his knees and icicles hang from his beard,
But he is used to the cold.
What stops him from sitting indoors?
Cold may be borne but hunger is hard to bear.

Five Poems on Country Life

1

ON a lucky day the bundles of rice shoots are opened, *
Thunder rolls in the southern hills, it rains all night;
No lack of water this year for the paddy fields,
For see how the rising stream laps the little bridge.

2

WEEDING the fields by day, twisting thread at night,
Even the village children have their tasks,
And little boys too small to plough or weave

---

* To be transplanted.

Learn to grow melons below the mulberry trees.

3

PLOUGH and hoe set aside they are hard at work picking
   caltrops,
Their fingers red with blood, as haggard as ghosts;
Those too poor to buy land can only sow in the water,
But now a new tax has been levied on the lake.

4

MEN sweat and strain before the harvest time,
Afraid of wind and rain, still more fearful of frost.
They beg Heaven to spare their crops,
For half must go to pay debts, half to the official.

5

THE newly made threshing-floor is as smooth as a mirror,
Each household is threshing rice on this clear, frosty night.
Through the laughter and singing sounds something like dis-
   tant thunder
As flails rattle on until the break of day.

XIN QIJI

Xin Qiji (1140-1207) was born in Ji'nan, Shandong after the Nüzhen Tartars occupied North China. The government of the Southern Song then in Hangzhou, eager to win a respite, signed a humiliating peace treaty in 1141. Xin joined the fighting to resist the invaders when he was twenty-two and later held a number of minor official posts. He presented memorials urging the throne to despatch an expedition against the Tartars but these were ignored.

He wrote more than six hundred poems in the *ci* form, many of which voice his lofty ideals and his concern at the fate of his country. His bold, unconstrained style exerted a significant influence on many later poets.

I Climb Shangxin Pavilion in Jiankang

— to the melody *Shui Long Yin*

A southern sky and a clear sweep of autumn,

Water brims to the skyline, autumn knows no bounds,

While the distant hills,

Jade clasps on a girl's coiled tresses,

Only conjure up grief and pain.

High in the pavilion I watch the setting sun,

Hear the cry of a lonely swan,

A wanderer in the south, gazing at my sword,

I beat time on the balustrade,

With none to know

What passes through my mind.

True, this is the season for perch,

But will the west wind

Blow the wanderer home?*

Those who grub for houses and land

Must blush to meet a noble-hearted man.**

Ah, the years slip past

---

* An allusion to Zhang Han, a scholar of the Jin Dynasty (A. D. 265-420), who gave up his office to return home when he saw it was autumn and the time to eat perch in the Yangtse Valley.

** At the end of the Han Dynasty (206 B. C.-A. D. 220) Chen Deng ignored Xu Fan because the latter was only interested in looking for good properties to buy, regardless of the fate of the empire.

Lamented by wind and rain,

And even the trees grow old!

Who will summon a green-sleeved maid

With red handkerchief

To wipe the hero's tears?

Written on the Wall at Zaokou in Jiangxi

— to the melody *Pu Sa Man*

PAST Yugu Tower flows the Qing

Bearing the tears of countless wayfarers,

And I gaze northwest towards Chang'an

Dismayed by all the hills that lie between.

Green mountains are no bar

To the Qing flowing on to the sea,

But as dusk falls on the stream my heart is heavy

When I hear the cuckoos calling deep in the hills.

On the Way to Dongyang

— to the melody *Zhe Gu Tian*

DUST wafts in my face, the road recedes behind

And the ambergris dwindles in my scented pouch;

Turquoise-green the countless hills on every side,

Rare the loveliness of these flowers unknown to me.

A sprinkling of riders, a whinnying of horses,
And now their banner has crossed the small red bridge.
To dispel my listlessness I make a verse
And flourish my whip with its handle of green jade.

Written on the Birthday of the Minister Han Nanjian in the Year Jiachen[*]

— to the melody Shui Long Yin

SINCE the emperor crossed the Yangtse and rode south[**]
There have been few true men of worth.
While the elders waited in Chang'an
Those recreants enjoyed the scenery of Xinting,[***]
Lamenting that year after year it remained unchanged.
Now worthless ministers
Have ruined our sacred land,
Yet seldom do their eyes turn towards the north;
The conquest of the Tartar hordes ten thousand li away,
As you, sir, know,

---

* 1184.
** In 1126 Kaifeng fell to the Tartars and the Song court moved south.
*** In the fourth century the Jin court moved south of the Yangtse to establish the Eastern Jin Dynasty. Officials used to gather in Xinting to enjoy the scenery and to lament their lost territory in the north.

Is a task left to us scholars.

You are far above us in learning

As Mount Tai or the Pole-star,

And plane trees shake

Your quiet, secluded court.

We can see your swift advance

Since you came to this earth,

Swift as clouds swept by the wind.

Yours now are the wind and mist of Lüye, *

The trees and herbs of Pingquan,

The wine and songs of Dongshan.

In time to come

When order is restored,

I shall drink to your birthday again.

A Night in Wang's Hut at Boshan

— to the melody *Qing Ping Yue*

FAMISHED rats scuffle round the bed,

Bats flit round the lamp,

Wind from the pines lashes the roof with rain

---

* Lüye was the name of a villa belonging to Pei Du, a prime minister of the Tang
Dynasty. Pingquan was another Tang minister Li Deyu's villa. Dongshan was a
place frequented by the Jin minister Xie An. These three men were all distinguished statesmen of the past.

And torn window paper whispers to itself.

All my life I have travelled north and south
And am now returned whiteheaded, my face haggard;
Waking under my cotton quilt this autumn night
I still see our magnificent land stretching to infinity.

Written on the Wall on My Way to Boshan
— to the melody *Chou Nu Er*

AS a lad I never knew the taste of sorrow,
But loved to climb towers,
Loved to climb towers,
And drag sorrow into each new song I sung.
Now I know well the taste of sorrow,
It is on the tip of my tongue,
On the tip of my tongue,
But instead I say, "What a fine, cool autumn day!"

The Lantern Festival
— to the melody *Qing Yu An*

IN the east wind tonight a thousand trees burst into bloom
And stars are blown down like rain;
The whole perfumed road is thronged

With fine carriages and horses bright with gems;

Phoenix flutes make music,

The jade clepsydra flashes,

Fish and dragon lanterns whirl the whole night long.

Golden willow and butterfly trinkets in her hair,

Laughing and chatting she leaves a faint fragrance behind
  her;

A thousand times I search for her in the crowd

And, suddenly turning my head,

Discover her where the lantern lights are dim.

Life in the Village

— to the melody *Qing Ping Yue*

THE eaves of the thatched hut hang low,

Green, green the grass by the stream:

What tipsy white-haired couple have we here

Billing and cooing in accents of the south?

Their first-born is hoeing the bean plot east of the stream,

The second is making a hen coop;

Their best-loved, youngest scamp

Sprawled out on the bank is peeling lotus seeds.

To Chen Liang

— to the melody *He Xin Lang*

Chen Liang came from Dongyang and stayed with me for ten days. I took him to visit Goose Lake and we arranged to see Zhu Xi at Zixi, but he did not come and my friend had to go back east. The day after his departure I missed him so much that I started out after him. In E-gret Wood, however, the snow was too deep and the path too slippery for me to go on. I did some solitary drinking in Fang Village and remained for a long time depressed by my failure to bring him back. Late that night I found lodgings in Siwang Pavilion belonging to the Wu family in Quanhu, and the plaintive fluting from the next house made me pour out my feelings in a song written to the tune Ru Yan Fei. Five days later a letter came from Chen Liang asking me for a poem. It is rather amusing that far apart as we were both of us were thinking along similar lines.

CUP in hand we talked before parting,
You a second Tao Yuanming*
High-hearted as sagacious Zhuge Liang.**
From the wood came flitting a magpie
Scattering flakes of snow from the pine branches
To add white to the hair
Below our tattered hats.
Dwindling stream and meagre hills were not much to look
   at,

---

* The great fifth-century poet who gave up a government post and chose to live as a hermit.

** A statesman of the third century who made repeated attempts to regain the central Chinese plain.

Barely making a picture with sparse branches of plum,
And the few wild-geese winging past
Seemed lonely too.

My friend kept tryst but left me all too soon;
I gaze disconsolately at the Qing,
Too cold to be forded today,
Deep and packed with ice.
The road is cut, cart-wheels bog down in ruts,
Causing grief to the traveller!
Who sent you, friend,
To rend my heart like this?
All the iron on earth was surely spent
To forge so great a weight of pain and longing;
Beware lest it shatter the flute
This long, slow night.

A Poem in a Heroic Vein for Chen Liang

— to the melody *Po Zhen Zi*

HALF drunk I lit the lamp to look at my sword
After dreams of the bugling in our army camps,
The roasted oxen shared among our men,
The harpist's melody from the northern border.
It was autumn, we marshalled our troops on the field of
    war.

Horses sped as if on wings,
Bow-strings twanged like thunder,

And we carried out the emperor's behest
Winning fame both in life and in death...
But now, alas, my hair is turning white!

Huangsha Ridge

— to the melody *Huan Xi Sha*

ON a small plot of land stands a tower a hundred feet high;
Lone fort, spring flood, a solitary seagull,
And the winds of heaven buffet the trees unceasingly.

Rocks loom sudden and fierce before men,
Shy flowers lurk half-hidden by the roadside,
And east of the temple by the stream is a cottage.

Travelling at Night to Huangsha Ridge

— to the melody *Xi Jiang Yue*

THE bright moon startles the crow on the slanting bough,
At midnight the breeze is cool, cicadas shrill;
The fragrance of the paddy foretells a good year
And frogs croak far and wide.

Seven or eight stars at the horizon,
Two or three drops of rain before the hill;
An old thatched inn borders the wood with the local shrine,
And where the road bends a small bridge is suddenly seen.

A Poem

— to the melody *Zhe Gu Tian*

Written in jest when a friend's impassioned talk of achievement and fame made me think back to my youth

IN my youth ten thousand men flocked to my standard,
In brocade coats we galloped north and crossed the Yangtse;
The Tartars at night checked their quivers inlaid with silver,
Our men in the morning shot arrows tipped with gold.

I long for the past and grieve over my present state,
What spring wind can turn my white beard black again?
In place of memorials on destroying the Tartars
I read my neighbour's manual on growing trees!

For a Friend

— to the melody *Zhe Gu Tian*

THE roadside mulberries break into tender leaf,
Our east neighbour's silkworm eggs are hatching out;
A brown calf lows on the gentle, grassy slope,
Dusky crows dot the chill wood as the sun slants down.

Hills near and far,
A winding road,
And under the blue pennon a wine tavern;

The peach and plum in town fear the wind and rain,
But spring has come to the fountain where the shepherd's
   purse is in bloom.

Written for Fun

— to the melody *Xi Jiang Yue*

IN my cups I want nothing but fun and jollity,
What time have I for care?
Of late I begin to see the futility
Of trusting in those books by the men of old.

Last night by the pine I staggered tipsily
And asked the pine, "How drunk am I?"
When I imagined the pine sidling over to support me,
I pushed it off saying, "Away!"

Sights on a Trip to Changshan

— to the melody *Huan Xi Sha*

ON the north bank the fields are high, tread-wheels are
   pumping water;
By the west stream the crops ripen early, already they have
   eaten new rice;
I buy wine from next door and cook a fine-scaled fish.

A breath of cool air — it must have rained near by —

But in a flash the shadows of the clouds are gone
And a melon-vendor passes the village by the bamboos.

Thinking of the Past at Beigu Pavilion in Jingkou

— to the melody *Yong Yu Le*

IN this ancient land
What trace remains of Wu's brave king Sun Quan?*
Towers and pavilions where girls danced and sang,
Your glory is swept away by wind and rain;
The slanting sunlight falls on grass and trees,
Small lanes, the quarters of the humble folk;
Yet here, they say, Liu Yu** lived.
I think of the days gone by
When with gilded spear and iron-clad steed he charged
Like a tiger to swallow up vast territories.
In the days of Yuanjia***
Hasty preparations were made
To march to the Langjuxu Mountains,****
But the men of Song were routed from the north.
Now forty-three years have passed,
And looking north I remember

---

  * A third-century king who reigned in Jingkou.
 ** The first ruler of the Southern Song Dynasty in the fifth century and a native of this city, who led successful expeditions against the northern Tartars.
*** A.D. 424-453.
**** In Inner Mongolia, reached by the Han army after defeating the Huns in 119 B.C.

The beacon fires that blazed the way to Yangzhou; *
Bitter memories these
Of sacred crows among the holy drums
In the Tartar emperor's temple, **

Who will ask old Lian Po***
If he still enjoys his food?

Thoughts in Beigu Pavilion at Jingkou

— to the melody *Nan Xiang Zi*

WHERE can I see our northern territory?
Splendid the view from the Beigu Pavilion.
How many dynasties have risen and fallen
In the course of long centuries,
And history goes on
Endless as the swift-flowing Yangtse.
A young king**** with a host of armoured men
Held the southeast and fought with never a moment's
    respite;

---

* In 1161 the Nüzhen Tartars occupied Yangzhou.

** When Northern Wei, a Tartar dynasty, defeated the Southern Song troops in the
fifth century, their emperor built a temple near Yangzhou.

*** A brave general of the Warring States period (475-221 B.C.), who to prove his
ability to lead an army in his old age rode out in full armour after a hearty meal.

**** Referring to Sun Quan who founded the kingdom of Wu in the third century after
the break-up of the Han empire. Wu occupied the lower reaches of the Yangtse;
Shu, ruled by Liu Bei, was in the upper Yangtse Valley and Sichuan; while north
China was ruled by Cao Cao, whose son founded the kingdom of Wei.

Two alone of all the empire's heroes could match him —
Brave Cao Cao and Liu Bei.
"How I long for a son like Sun Quan!" *

An Inscription for Chenpiao Pavilion at Jingkou

— to the melody *Sheng Zha Zi*

GREAT deeds live on ten thousand generations:
Hard he toiled in ancient times
That fish might plunge in the vast deep
And men dwell on the plain.

The red sun sets once more in the west,
White billows surge endlessly east;
My eyes are not fixed on the Mount of Gold
But my thoughts turn to King Yu. **

---

* A remark made by Cao Cao.
** The legendary pacifier of flood.

图书在版编目（CIP）数据

唐宋诗文选/（唐）李白等著；杨宪益，戴乃迭译．－北京：外文出版社，
2003.11
（熊猫丛书）
ISBN 7-119-03355-7

Ⅰ．唐... Ⅱ．①李...②杨...③戴... Ⅲ．英语－语言读物，古典文学
Ⅳ．H319.4：Ⅰ

中国版本图书馆 CIP 数据核字（2003）第 055136 号

外文出版社网址：
　http://www.flp.com.cn
外文出版社电子信箱：
　info@flp.com.cn
　sales@flp.com.cn

熊猫丛书

唐宋诗文选

作　　者	李　白等	
译　　者	杨宪益　戴乃迭	
责任编辑	陈海燕　李　芳	
封面设计	唐少文	
印刷监制	张国祥	
出版发行	外文出版社	
社　　址	北京市百万庄大街 24 号	邮政编码　100037
电　　话	（010）68320579（总编室）	
	（010）68329514/68327211（推广发行部）	
印　　刷	北京中印联印务有限公司	
经　　销	新华书店/外文书店	
开　　本	大 32 开	
印　　数	2001—4000 册	印　张　9.375
版　　次	2006 年第 1 版第 2 次印刷	
装　　别	平	
书　　号	ISBN 7-119-03355-7	
	10—E—3566P	
定　　价	26.00 元	